Sharing Higher Education's Promise beyond the Few in Sub-Saharan Africa

DIRECTIONS IN DEVELOPMENT
Human Development

Sharing Higher Education's Promise beyond the Few in Sub-Saharan Africa

Peter Darvas, Shang Gao, Yijun Shen, and Bilal Bawany

© 2017 International Bank for Reconstruction and Development / The World Bank
1818 H Street NW, Washington, DC 20433
Telephone: 202-473-1000; Internet: www.worldbank.org

Some rights reserved

1 2 3 4   20 19 18 17

This work is a product of the staff of The World Bank with external contributions. The findings, interpretations, and conclusions expressed in this work do not necessarily reflect the views of The World Bank, its Board of Executive Directors, or the governments they represent. The World Bank does not guarantee the accuracy of the data included in this work. The boundaries, colors, denominations, and other information shown on any map in this work do not imply any judgment on the part of The World Bank concerning the legal status of any territory or the endorsement or acceptance of such boundaries.

Nothing herein shall constitute or be considered to be a limitation upon or waiver of the privileges and immunities of The World Bank, all of which are specifically reserved.

Rights and Permissions

This work is available under the Creative Commons Attribution 3.0 IGO license (CC BY 3.0 IGO) http://creativecommons.org/licenses/by/3.0/igo. Under the Creative Commons Attribution license, you are free to copy, distribute, transmit, and adapt this work, including for commercial purposes, under the following conditions:

Attribution—Please cite the work as follows: Darvas, Peter, Shang Gao, Yijun Shen, and Bilal Bawany. 2017. *Sharing Higher Education's Promise beyond the Few in Sub-Saharan Africa*. Directions in Development. Washington, DC: World Bank. doi:10.1596/978-1-4648-1050-3. License: Creative Commons Attribution CC BY 3.0 IGO

Translations—If you create a translation of this work, please add the following disclaimer along with the attribution: *This translation was not created by The World Bank and should not be considered an official World Bank translation. The World Bank shall not be liable for any content or error in this translation.*

Adaptations—If you create an adaptation of this work, please add the following disclaimer along with the attribution: *This is an adaptation of an original work by The World Bank. Views and opinions expressed in the adaptation are the sole responsibility of the author or authors of the adaptation and are not endorsed by The World Bank.*

Third-party content—The World Bank does not necessarily own each component of the content contained within the work. The World Bank therefore does not warrant that the use of any third-party-owned individual component or part contained in the work will not infringe on the rights of those third parties. The risk of claims resulting from such infringement rests solely with you. If you wish to re-use a component of the work, it is your responsibility to determine whether permission is needed for that re-use and to obtain permission from the copyright owner. Examples of components can include, but are not limited to, tables, figures, or images.

All queries on rights and licenses should be addressed to World Bank Publications, The World Bank Group, 1818 H Street NW, Washington, DC 20433, USA; e-mail: pubrights@worldbank.org.

ISBN (paper): 978-1-4648-1050-3
ISBN (electronic): 978-1-4648-1051-0
DOI: 10.1596/978-1-4648-1050-3

Cover photo: © Albert González Farran/UNAMID. Used with the permission of UNAMID; further permission required for reuse.
Cover design: Debra Naylor, Naylor Design, Inc.

Library of Congress Cataloging-in-Publication Data has been requested.

Contents

Foreword		*ix*
Acknowledgments		*xi*
Overview		*xiii*
Abbreviations		*xix*
Chapter 1	**Introduction**	1
	Equity in Education	1
	Context and Purpose	1
	Structure of This Book	6
	Key Definitions	7
	References	9
Chapter 2	**Supply and Demand**	11
	Key Messages	11
	Growth in Supply	11
	Diversification of Supply	12
	Demand and Economic Development	15
	Economic Structure and Diversification	17
	Growth in Pre-Tertiary Enrollment	21
	Note	23
	References	23
Chapter 3	**Equity Patterns**	25
	Key Messages	25
	Socioeconomic Status	25
	Gender	28
	Parents' Education	30
	Spatial and Regional Factors	31
	Students with Disabilities	31
	References	32
Chapter 4	**Equity of Opportunities**	35
	Key Messages	35
	Inequity in Pre-Tertiary Levels of Education	35
	Costs of Pursuing Tertiary Education	40

	Government Expenditures	44
	Benefit Incidence Analysis	48
	Tertiary Admissions Policies	51
	Notes	52
	References	52
Chapter 5	**Equity of Outcomes**	**55**
	Key Messages	55
	Private Returns to Tertiary Education	55
	Public Returns to Tertiary Education	59
	Social Returns to Tertiary Education	60
	Social Mobility and Tertiary Education	61
	References	63
Chapter 6	**Government Policies to Address Inequity**	**65**
	Key Messages	65
	Country Policy and Institutional Assessment	66
	Admissions Policy Initiatives	68
	Bridge Programs	69
	Financial Aid	70
	Diversification	72
	Budget Management	74
	Innovative Financing for Higher Education	74
	References	75
Chapter 7	**In-Depth Country Case Studies**	**79**
	Introduction	79
	The Case of Ghana	79
	The Case of Guinea	83
	The Case of Kenya	84
	The Case of Malawi	85
	The Case of Mozambique	86
	The Case of Niger	87
	The Case of Nigeria	88
	The Case of Senegal	89
	The Case of Sierra Leone	90
	The Case of Uganda	92
	References	92
Appendix	**List of Countries for Which Household Survey Data Are Available**	**95**

Box

5.1	Does Higher Educational Attainment Lead to Higher Private Returns? The Case of the Democratic Republic of Congo	57

Figures

2.1	Gross Enrollment Ratio, by Region, 1970–2013	12
2.2	Share of Tertiary Enrollment in Private Institutions, 2000 and 2012	13
2.3	Number of Tertiary Students per 100,000 Inhabitants versus Share of Students Enrolled in Private Higher Education, 2012	14
2.4	Share of Short-Cycle Tertiary Education in Total Tertiary Education, 2012	15
2.5	Enrollment in Short-Cycle Tertiary Education versus Overall Tertiary Enrollment	15
2.6	Tertiary Enrollment per 100,000 Inhabitants and GDP per Capita (Current US$), 2013	16
2.7	Economic Structure by Employment, Latest Household Survey	17
2.8	Share of Manufacturing and Services Employment	19
2.9	Tertiary GER and the Share of Employees with Tertiary Education in the Public Sector	20
2.10	Upper-Secondary Education GER and Growth Rate, 2000 and 2012	22
2.11	Senior Secondary and Tertiary GER	22
3.1	Distribution of Income or Consumption, by Quintile	26
3.2	Tertiary Education GER by Wealth Quintiles, by Sub-Saharan African Region	26
3.3	Gross Enrollment Ratio for Postsecondary Education for African Countries	27
3.4	Gross Enrollment Ratio, Gender Parity Index, and Tertiary Education	28
3.5	Tertiary GER Gender Parity Index in Selected Countries, 2000 and 2012	29
3.6	Tertiary GER by Head of Household's Educational Attainment	30
4.1	Mean Years of Schooling for Population Ages 15–64 Years, Top 20 Percent versus Bottom 80 Percent, by Income	37
4.2	Inequity of Educational Attainment, 1990–2010	38
4.3	Education Attainment Inequality Index and Tertiary Enrollment per 100,000 Inhabitants in Selected Sub-Saharan African Countries	38
4.4	Student Composition in Terms of Family Wealth Condition from Preschool to Tertiary-Level Education	39
4.5	Education Expenditures as a Percentage of Household Non–Food-Related Expenditures	42
4.6	Education and Private Income	43
4.7	Share of Government Spending, by Level of Education	44
4.8	Public Expenditures per Tertiary Student over the Costs of Educating One Student in Primary School, SSA and Countries with Similar Profile	45
4.9	Ratio of Current Public Expenditures per Tertiary Student to Current Public Expenditures per Primary Student, SSA versus Non-SSA Countries	46

4.10	Recurrent Expenditures as a Percentage of Total Expenditures in Tertiary Public Institutions	47
4.11	Total Salaries as a Share of Total Expenditures in Tertiary Public Institutions, Selected SSA Countries	48
4.12	Outbound Mobility Ratio, 2013	49
4.13	Lorenz Curves for Incidence of Public Expenditures in Tertiary Education in Ghana, Mali, Rwanda, Tanzania, and Uganda	50
B5.1.1	Summary of Returns to Education	58
B5.1.2	Returns to Education, by Province	59
5.1	A Classification of Market and Nonmarket Benefits of Education	60
5.2	Earning Differences, by Education Level and Income Groups	62
5.3	Earning Differences of the Bottom 40 Percent, by Levels of Education	63
6.1	Equity of Public Resource Use and Tertiary Enrollment per 100,000 Inhabitants	67
6.2	Country Policy and Institutional Assessment on Gender Equality and Tertiary Enrollment per 100,000 Inhabitants	68
7.1	Benefit Incidence at Different Levels of Education	81
7.2	Average Household Spending on Education, by Income Quintile	82

Tables

4.1	Student Composition in Terms of Family Wealth Condition from Primary- to Tertiary-Level Education	40
4.2	Education Gini Coefficients in Ghana, Mali, Tanzania, and Malawi	50
5.1	Average Returns to Schooling, by Education Level and Gender	56
B5.1.1	Average Schooling Statistics in the Democratic Republic of Congo	57
B5.1.2	Estimated Opportunity Cost, by Level of Education	58
6.1	Student Loan Schemes in Sub-Saharan Africa	71
7.1	Tertiary Education Indicators in Selected SSA Countries	80
7.2	Income Levels (Hourly FCFA) Dependent on Education and Professional Category	88

Foreword

In 2016, economic growth in the Sub-Saharan Africa (SSA) region reached the weakest pace in over two decades as a result of the low commodity prices that affect many economies in the region with strong reliance on mining and production of other raw materials. Against the backdrop of slow growth, it is even more important for SSA countries to diversify their economies, improve productivity, build value chains for agriculture, and improve both domestic and export markets. Because knowledge is the driver of productivity and economic growth, these goals require building human capital through more accessible, equitable, and better-quality education and training systems. The demographic challenge of a fast-growing youth population in the SSA region is where the opportunity lies, if SSA countries can effectively equip an expanding pool of youth with access to education, endow them with cognitive, socioemotional and technical skills, and create conducive environment for job-creating businesses. SSA countries are increasingly looking at education especially tertiary education for such knowledge provision.

The increasing demand and limited supply of tertiary education in the SSA region has led to tertiary education being available only to a subset of the youth population. As the upcoming World Bank regional report *The Skills Balancing Act in Sub-Saharan Africa: Investing in Skills for Productivity, Inclusion, and Adaptability*[1] points out, "international experience suggests that university education often starts being biased towards the elite and as it expands it becomes more equitable, albeit rarely without distinct policies aimed at achieving this." Indeed, in SSA, the selection process has remained based on persistent social inequities and disparities by gender, geography, and ethnicity. To date, tertiary education in SSA region has remained elitist, benefiting students mostly from the most affluent, well-connected families. Coupled with the "brain drain" phenomena that talented tertiary graduates leave SSA regions after they finish education, tertiary education in the region is not equitably producing the human capital that the countries direly need.

In 2000, the Task Force on Higher Education and Society, convened by UNESCO and the World Bank, laid out the new realities, the public interest, and the systemic agenda as well as the challenges that higher education was facing, in a seminal report, *Higher Education in Developing Countries: Peril and Promise*.[2] Two decades later, there are not only new global opportunities but also persistent challenges that tertiary education systems face. In the meantime, the stakes have increased for SSA with unprecedented population growth, democratic transition, peace dividend, and economic transition. It is important thus to have a good understanding of how the tertiary education systems in the SSA region can fulfill their roles in spurring economic growth by expanding themselves to a wider range of students, whether such expansion will truly lead to more equitable result, and what the policy makers' roles are in the process. The book *Sharing Higher Education's Promise beyond the Few in Sub-Saharan Africa* addresses these concerns and provides insights into the transformative potential of tertiary education in the region for more equitable societies.

Jaime Saavedra Chanduvi
Senior Director
Education Global Practice
World Bank Group

Notes

1. Forthcoming in 2018.
2. Available at http://documents.worldbank.org/curated/en/345111467989458740/pdf/multi-page.pdf.

Acknowledgments

The authors thank Jaime Saavedra Chanduvi, Amit Dar, and Luis Benveniste (Directors); and Peter Nicolas Materu, Meskerem Mulatu, and Halil Dundar (Managers) of the World Bank Group's Education Global Practice for their overall leadership and management guidance. The authors also thank Andreas Blom, Emanuela Di Gropello, Francisco Marmolejo, and Michael Crawford for peer reviews and technical guidance.

The teams working on the prior research and on this book received significant support, input on background analysis, and advice from many colleagues, including Atou Seck, Dave Evans, Futoshi Yamauchi, Halsey Rogers, Hiroshi Saeki, Jamil Salmi, Kebede Feda, Omar Arias, Pierre Kamano, Mariam Nusrat Adil, and Sonali Ballal. Editing and publishing support were provided by Jonathan Faull, Aziz Gökdemir, and Rumit Pancholi. Janet Adebo provided invaluable administrative support throughout the process.

Overview

The Demand for Tertiary Education

In an increasingly globalized world, characterized by a growing knowledge economy, it is imperative for countries to identify and build comparative advantage in economic sectors that demonstrate potential for generating sustainable and job-producing growth. Concurrently, countries must innovate and produce new technologies to catalyze their comparative advantage and adapt technologies to address local challenges. The role of higher education in Sub-Saharan Africa (SSA) in supporting and producing these outcomes is critical: through the inculcation of job-relevant skills aligned with demand in the economy; through the promotion of skills to complement the development of competitive advantage; and as the locus of learning, innovation, and the production and adaptation of technologies.

In the recent past, tertiary systems of education in SSA have undergone significant expansion. In 1970, there were fewer than 400,000 tertiary students in the region, whereas in 2013 gross enrollment in higher education in the countries of SSA was approximately 7.2 million. Over the same period, the gross enrollment ratio (GER) for tertiary education grew at an average annual rate of 4.3 percent, compared with a global average of 2.8 percent.

On the supply side, public universities have significantly expanded their capacity to accommodate rising enrollment. However, the improved supply of tertiary education has also been driven by a diversification of suppliers and the recent spectacular expansion of private tertiary education provision. As the market increasingly demands readily employable graduates, short-cycle education programs have flourished, contributing to an improved supply of vocationally trained workers to the economies of the region.

Through the course of the past decade, the majority of countries in SSA have demonstrated strong and sustained economic growth and increasing demand from the private sector for more sophisticated forms of human capital and skilled labor. In 2014, 4 of the 10 fastest-growing economies in the world were in the SSA region. Contemporary growth has been underpinned by improved macroeconomic stability, the implementation of reforms to address market failures and improve market efficiency, the reduction of trade barriers, and, most consequentially, booming demand for commodities. In the immediate term, a slowdown in the Chinese economy, reduced global demand for commodities, infrastructure and electricity supply bottlenecks, and poor diversification of sources of economic growth have slowed short-term growth projections. Notwithstanding these challenges, year-on-year growth in the economies of SSA was expected to increase to 3.4 percent in 2015, and is projected by the World Bank to rise to 4.2 percent in 2016 and 4.7 percent in 2017.

The imperative to achieve further economic diversification, and to upgrade technology and competitiveness in the manufacturing and services sectors, will continue to drive improved demand for workers with postprimary qualifications and job-relevant skills. Concurrently, improved GERs in primary and secondary cycles of education, associated with interventions by regional governments to achieve the education-related Millennium Development Goals, have increased significantly the volume of students demanding higher education. The Organisation for Economic Co-operation and Development projects that improved enrollment in primary education will result in 59 percent of the region's 20 to 24-year-old adults—equivalent to 137 million people—holding a secondary education qualification by 2030, compared to just 42 percent today (AfDB and others 2012).

Despite a spectacular expansion of the higher education sector in SSA, the supply of tertiary education has generally failed to keep pace with demand, and the region continues to lag behind all others in terms of access to tertiary education. This is in part a consequence of deeply entrenched patterns of inequitable access to higher education and the perpetuation of what researchers refer to as "elite systems."

The fact that SSA's labor force is projected to almost double to 1 billion by 2040 underlines the scale of the demographic challenge going forward and brings into sharp focus the need to expand access to quality tertiary education. In the absence of effective policies to equip workers with the skills they require to compete in the labor force, a rising tide of under- and unemployed youth has the potential to undermine social cohesion and to contribute to political instability. On the other hand, if the education system in general, and institutions of tertiary education specifically, can effectively endow an expanding pool of workers with skills and knowledge to improve their livelihoods, drive job-creating economic growth, and enhance economic competitiveness and productivity, the countries of SSA stand to benefit from a significant "demographic dividend."

To achieve these ends, the doors to higher education must be open to all worthy students, regardless of socioeconomic status, gender, and regional origin. Equitable systems of tertiary education have the potential to fundamentally transform societies by allowing traditionally underrepresented groups to participate more effectively in socioeconomic decision making. As a result, the equitable accumulation of tertiary education across a population leads to a more equitable distribution of resources and wealth. To date, access to tertiary education in SSA has unduly benefited students drawn from the region's wealthiest households, and overall enrollment remains disproportionately male and metropolitan. These factors stifle the catalytic potential of higher education, corroding its potential for driving economic growth and sustaining poverty reduction. Instead, patterns of access to tertiary education in SSA have generally reinforced and reproduced social inequality rather than eroding its pernicious social and economic effects.

Objectives

This book aims to inform an improved understanding of equity in tertiary enrollment in SSA countries and examine the extent to which inequity functions as a bottleneck, inhibiting the ability of African universities to effectively drive improvements in overall quality of life and economic competitiveness. In our survey of the evidence, we also aim to identify which policies most effectively address the challenge of promoting equity of access in SSA tertiary education systems. To achieve these objectives, the book collects, generates, and analyzes empirical evidence on patterns of inequity; examines its underlying causes; and evaluates government policies for addressing it.

Toward these ends, the book analyzes returns to tertiary education in SSA for both the individual and society, in market and nonmarket forms, and focuses on three types of returns to education: private, public, and social. *Private* rates of return to education are measured through a comparison of increases in an individual's income, associated with the completion of an additional year of schooling, or level of education, and the increased costs associated with further education. A recent, groundbreaking World Bank study (Montenegro and Patrinos 2014) of returns to education in 144 economies buttresses the case that private returns accruing to tertiary graduates in SSA are larger than those observed in other regions, and that these returns generally dwarf those associated with lower levels of education.

In addition to the analysis of private returns to education in SSA, this book measures *public* rates of return, computed by taking into account the public costs and benefits accruing to education provision. Public costs are those borne by society as a whole and include government spending, individual tuition, and opportunity cost, and benefits are based on pretax earnings instead of posttax earnings. As a consequence, this book uses comparative public returns to education as a means to measure and assess the efficiency of public spending on education.

Private returns are measured through a comparison of earnings between individuals who hold a tertiary qualification and those who do not. The difference between public and private returns is the inclusion of costs borne by the whole society in calculating public returns, and public returns are smaller than private returns because of the inclusion of these costs. Calculating *social* returns is both more complex and more difficult. Tertiary education contributes to improved health, comparatively well-educated children, and improved consumer efficiency at the individual level. At a societal level, improved access to tertiary education can increase tax revenue and economic growth through productivity-related externalities such as knowledge creation, research and development, improved public health, lower rates of crime, and improved social cohesion.

In an effort to isolate effective and suboptimal interventions to promote equity in systems of higher education, the book presents a trend analysis of equity in tertiary education in SSA complemented by 10 country case studies.

Key Findings

An analysis of the supply and demand of tertiary education in SSA demonstrates that, notwithstanding the significant increase in tertiary enrollment in the region, growth in the demand for tertiary education has far outpaced increased supply.

The book demonstrates that, despite a rapid growth in tertiary enrollment and, in some cases, improved access on the part of students from traditionally underserved groups, SSA tertiary education continues to perpetuate and mirror significant social inequity. Household wealth continues to constitute the most decisive factor in determining a students' chance of accessing tertiary education. Although gender parity has improved, the legacy of patriarchy continues to undermine equitable participation on the part of African female students, and gendered patterns of program choice are evident in enrollment data. Children born into families whose head of household holds a high school diploma are far more likely to enroll in tertiary education than children who, through the accident of birth, are born into households whose head of household has no education. Moreover, regional inequity, reinforced by spatial patterns of economic development concentrating the supply of tertiary education in urban areas, undermines participation on the part of students from rural and economically marginal communities.

The disparities in access to higher education examined in this book are myriad and complex. The majority of students who enroll in pre-tertiary levels of education in SSA exit the system before obtaining the qualifications necessary to inform a choice about enrolling in higher education. Children from comparatively poor households, as well as children in rural areas, are less likely to benefit from programs for early childhood education, and are less likely to enroll in primary education on time. These factors negatively impact the chances that a child will stay in school, and they contribute to comparatively high dropout rates among affected populations.

The pernicious effects of socioeconomic status privilege the children of the wealthy and politically connected. These children disproportionately and, from an equity perspective, regressively benefit from free and heavily subsidized systems of higher education because of better access to good schools capable of equipping them with skills for further education, access to academic role models, and other forms of cultural capital. Children from comparatively poor households are less likely to have access to information regarding admissions procedures and the relative merits of different programs of study, as well as accurate information regarding the labor market returns associated with different types of tertiary education.

Direct and indirect costs, such as the opportunity cost associated with pursuing tertiary education, further affect equity of access and privilege access on the part of students from comparatively wealthy households. If a household must cover the costs of fees and living expenses for a child to continue his or her studies, the impact of the associated burden on the disposable income of a poor household relative to a rich household is obvious. Moreover, opportunity costs associated with education weigh more heavily on low-income families because they must forgo the income of household members enrolled in education and because of the perception of poor labor market returns accruing to tertiary graduates in many economies of the region.

A further factor undermining equity of access to education in SSA is that in many instances public financing of tertiary education perpetuates inequity through its support of elite students, who are disproportionately sourced from urban and wealthy households. This is especially egregious in systems wherein public monies are used to support students who study abroad, many or most of whom will not return to their home countries. Finally, differences in the admissions policies of Francophone and Anglophone countries account, in part, for observed differences in equity outcomes.

The book demonstrates that increases in educational attainment are associated with increased income, with progressively higher jumps in earnings evident for upper-secondary and postsecondary graduates. In many countries, the earnings premium accruing to upper-secondary graduates is high, and they earn 100–150 percent more than people with no education. Although returns to education are largest at the tertiary level, the difference between private and public returns is much higher in SSA because of the magnitude of public costs. A potential benefit of tertiary education is its strong impact on social mobility, with the analysis suggesting that returns to higher education are largest for the poorest 40 percent of the population.

Increasing cost sharing on the part of tertiary institutions requires more effective financial aid policies to ensure improved access of underprivileged students to tertiary education. Governments increasingly use student loans to reduce the cost of financial aid, but not all student loans are means tested. In many instances, where means testing is used to inform loan decisions, the mechanisms used do not accurately establish the real family wealth of applicants. African countries generally have a poor track record of appraising and recovering student loans. Low loan recovery, in conjunction with low interest rates, results in almost all student loan programs requiring some level of public subsidization, in turn undermining the sustainability of these schemes.

The development of private universities increases the chance that students from disadvantaged backgrounds will access tertiary education. However, strong regulation is needed to address concerns regarding the quality of education delivered by private universities. Educational unit costs in the private sector are often much lower than those in the public sector, and as a consequence it is to the advantage of governments to encourage students to pursue training in the private sector, even if this requires public financial support.

The final section of this book details 10 country case studies to demonstrate how different tertiary education policies influence outcomes and patterns of equity or inequity. The selection of country case studies is based on the availability of data, including the extensive analyses of financing tertiary education published by the World Bank.

Data Sources

The analyses in this book are based on data drawn primarily from household surveys, including the Living Standards Measurement Study (LSMS) and Demographic and Health Surveys (DHS) carried out by the World Bank or the individual countries. A complete list of available household surveys is contained in the appendix of this book.

Other sources and databases used to inform the analysis contained in this book include the following::

- *Cisco Certified Internetwork Expert certification (CCIE)*: Cisco Certified Internetwork Expert certification (discontinued by COSCO).
- *Institute of International Education (IIE)*: Data on international students studying in the United States, http://www.iie.org.
- *International Telecommunications Union*: Telecom/information and communication technology indicators, http://www.itu.int/en/ITU-D/Statistics/Pages/default.aspx.
- *United Nations Educational, Scientific, and Cultural Organization (UNESCO) Institute for Statistics (UIS) database*: Various indicators related to education; science, technology, and innovation; culture; communication and information, demographic, and socioeconomic indexes; and the global mobility of international students, http://data.uis.unesco.org.
- *World Bank databases*: Country Policy and Institutional Assessment (CPIA), http://data.worldbank.org/data-catalog/CPIA; Education Statistics (EdStats), http://datatopics.worldbank.org/education/; and World Development Indicators (WDI), http://data.worldbank.org/data-catalog/world-development-indicators.
- *World Intellectual Property Organization*: Intellectual property indicators, http://www.wipo.int/portal/en/index.html.

References

AfDB, OECD, UNDP, and UNECA (African Development Bank, Organisation for Economic Co-operation and Development, United Nations Development Programme, and United Nations Economic Commission for Africa). 2012. *African Economic Outlook: Promoting Youth Employment*. Paris: OECD Publishing.

Montenegro, C. E., and H. A. Patrinos. 2014. "Comparable Estimates of Returns to Schooling around the World." Policy Research Working Paper 7020, World Bank, Washington, DC.

World Bank. 2011. *Rwanda—Education Country Status Report: Toward Quality Enhancement and Achievement of Universal Nine-Year Basic Education—An Education System in Transition*. Washington, DC: World Bank.

Abbreviations

ADB	Asian Development Bank
AfDB	African Development Bank
CCIE	Cisco Certified Internetwork Expert certification
CPIA	Country Policy and Institutional Assessment
DHS	Demographic and Health Surveys
GDP	gross domestic product
GER	gross enrollment ratio
HEI	higher education institution
HEST	Higher Education, Science and Technology Strategy
IDA	International Development Association
IIE	Institute of International Education
IMF	International Monetary Fund
ITU	International Telecommunications Union
KCPE	Kenya Certificate of Primary Education
KIST	Kigali Institute of Science, Technology, and Management (Rwanda)
KNUST	Kwame Nkrumah University of Science and Technology
LAY	latest available year
LES	less-endowed schools
LSMS	Living Standards Measurement Study
MDG	Millennium Development Goal
NSFAS	National Student Financial Aid Scheme
NUC	National Universities Commission
ODA	official development assistance
OECD	Organisation for Economic Co-operation and Development
PES	private entry scheme
PFM	public financial management
PHC	Population and Housing Census
PPBB	performance- and program-based budgeting
PRSP	Poverty Reduction Strategy Paper

PTR	pupil-teacher ratio
SARUA	Southern African Regional Universities Association
SLTF	Student Loan Trust Fund
SSA	Sub-Saharan Africa
STEM	science, technology, engineering, and mathematics
TVET	technical and vocational education and training
UIS	UNESCO Institute for Statistics
UNESCO	United Nations Educational, Scientific, and Cultural Organization
WASSCE	West African Senior School Certificate Examination

CHAPTER 1

Introduction

Equity in Education

There is a significant body of research that measures inequality in educational attainment across all levels of education. Clancy and Goastellec (2007), Ogawa and Iimura (2010), and Koucky, Bartusek, and Kovarovic (2010)—a subset of researchers focused on equity in higher education—assert that differences and commonalities between countries become evident through a comparative analysis of definitions of access and equity, and policies based on these definitions. However, comparative studies on inequitable access to, and inequitable attainment in, tertiary education across countries are rare, with the notable exception of Thomas, Wang, and Fan (2001), Zhang and Li (2002), Barros et al. (2009), and Koucky, Bartusek, and Kovarovic (2010). Research in this regard, with a specific focus on Sub-Saharan Africa (SSA), is even more difficult to come by. Examples of analytical work regarding challenges to tertiary education systems in SSA include the World Bank reports *Accelerating Catch-Up* (World Bank 2009) and *Financing Higher Education in Africa* (Experton and Fevre 2010); Varghese's (2004) research on private higher education; and Bloom, Canning, and Chan's (2006) study focusing on higher education and economic development. This book intends to fill some of the knowledge gap with regard to access and equity in tertiary education in SSA by collecting, generating, and analyzing empirical evidence on these indicators and, on the basis of this analysis, highlighting key policy entry points for addressing equity.

Context and Purpose

Who is the intended audience for this inquiry? The book aims to inform three broadly defined sets of actors: policy makers, analysts who inform policy making in government, and the community of researchers and stakeholders who are directly affected by changes in policy (students and their families, tertiary education staff, professionals and alumni, and the management of tertiary education institutions). Stakeholders, in this context, are deliberately defined as a broad constituency, inclusive of those who may be affected indirectly by changes in policy. This can be through the contributions of taxpayers; the effects of the higher education sector's relationship with, and impact on, the education system at large; labor markets; and social, demographic, and economic trends (including, for instance, social inclusion, poverty alleviation, migration, health outcomes, employment, productivity, and private sector growth).

Are tertiary education systems by definition inequitable? To what extent is inequity in tertiary education inevitable? How long does it take for these systems to reach a sufficient scale at which inequitable effects become less obvious? Is it important to identify specific patterns in, sources of, and the impact of inequity? Do short- or medium-term interventions exist that can effectively address inequity? The evidence presented in this book, while providing substantive, rich insights into each question, offers mixed results and does not allow for broadly applicable conclusions. This suggests that, unfortunately, there are no easy answers to these questions.

There is, for example, a certain inevitability that elite systems of education will reproduce some forms of inequity. However, the picture is more mixed in countries and regions in which higher education systems have been transformed through persistent expansion and diversification. This evidence suggests that some forms of inequity may be addressed only in the long term through deliberate and consistent policies and interventions. Such policies are not limited to supply-side interventions but also include actions and strategies deployed to influence social, economic, and employment outcomes—with a strategic focus on private sector development and job creation. The confluence of these sectors and energies affects the scope and scale of the benefits, the potential returns, and the mobility of individuals who must choose between tertiary study and early entry into the labor market.

How is the objective of achieving equity in tertiary education different from the pursuit of equity in education more generally? Numerous studies demonstrate that education systems characterized by greater equity reproduce and strengthen broader patterns of social and economic equity and social inclusion. Other studies (which we will revisit) suggest that inequities in systems of pre-tertiary education strongly impact patterns of inequity in tertiary education. The particularities of inequity at the tertiary level are also influenced by the increased out-of-pocket costs and higher opportunity costs associated with higher education. Individuals, families, and communities must weigh these costs in making decisions about accessing higher education. Concurrently, tertiary education is associated with improved employability, economic mobility, and higher earnings. In other words, the risks and opportunities associated with tertiary education are much greater than those presented in pre-tertiary cycles of education, especially for students from comparatively poor or underserved backgrounds.

Given the abundance of existing work on equity in tertiary education, why does this book collect more data and empirical evidence to demonstrate trends in inequality and produce more analysis? As public debate with regard to access to, and equity in, tertiary education in Africa intensifies, it is increasingly important to use empirical evidence to accurately inform stakeholders about patterns of equity and underlying causes of inequity, and to frame the policy implications of these trends. This book primarily uses data collected through surveys of representative samples of households. In some instances, the analysis contained in this book is able to draw on surveys administered over a meaningful period of time, uses comparable definitions, and therefore demonstrates high standards of reliability. Although it is true that, in general, insufficiently reliable and comparable data exist to build complex econometric models for analyzing outcomes and trends across SSA's systems of tertiary education, there is sufficient empirical information to reliably inform public debate and to monitor the results of government interventions in the sector. This study combines and compares data drawn from different administrative, cross-country data sources; country-specific and sample-based population and household surveys; and other relevant empirical analyses. Ultimately, we hope to demonstrate the utility of using reliable quantitative and qualitative information to inform higher education policy.

Why do we need to analyze patterns of inequity? It is important to analyze patterns and sources of inequity, as well as the effect of inequity on broader social and economic development trends, because it is this broader social tableau that tertiary education aims to serve. Locating the patterns, and the sources, of inequity can inform and improve education policy making so as to more effectively address associated challenges. The analyses in this book demonstrate important variations in country-level patterns of inequity within and beyond the SSA region. This implies that some countries and tertiary education institutions have more effective policies for addressing equity-related challenges—such as bottlenecks faced by poor families and communities, marginalized regions or ethnic groups, inequitable access by gender, or simple informational asymmetry (more or better information about the value of participating in tertiary education)—than others. Countries that do better in establishing and implementing policies to address these and other challenges appear to be relatively more successful at addressing broader economic and social concerns, although our analyses are not equipped to demonstrate this causality with empirical evidence (that is, the extent to which relatively equitable education has a clear effect on broader development, economic growth, social inclusion, productivity, or access to jobs).

Tertiary education is critical for human capital development. The work of Schultz (1961), Becker (1993), and Mincer (1974) informs the foundational theory of human capital. This theory contends that education constitutes an investment in an individual's human capital, which allows an individual to productively contribute to his or her society. This book does not revisit these, or subsequent, theories in detail because the current debate regarding human capital, and human capital formation, is largely settled.

The importance of equitable access to tertiary education is also well established for informing improved economic growth, poverty reduction, lower levels of underemployment, greater levels of civic participation, and improved public health in SSA (Bloom, Canning, and Chang 2006; Salmi et al. 2002). Moreover, equity in tertiary education is also seen as contributing to improving a country's capacity to absorb external aid (Walenkamp and Boeren 2007). In the absence of a robust and competitive private sector, effective tertiary education systems in developing countries play an important role in improving technological capacity, enhancing skills, and advancing entrepreneurship. The recognition of these and other benefits accruing to effectively operating equitable systems of tertiary education is increasingly widespread, and associated support to tertiary education by governments and development agencies, including the World Bank, appears to be steadily increasing.

After SSA's wave of independence, higher education was considered essential for cultivating human capital for effective leadership and governance. Newly independent governments invested heavily in education and training, leading to a rapid expansion in enrollment in the 1960s and 1970s across almost all SSA countries. However, after the first oil crisis in the early 1970s and the subsequent collapse of many African economies caused by the concurrent effects of corruption and increasing indiscipline in public budget management, many African universities faced significant strain, with negative implications for their management and performance (Devarajan, Monga, and Zongo 2011).

In the 1980s, the World Bank sponsored studies demonstrating greater rates of return to investments in education at lower levels of education, leading to the allocation of more funding to pre-tertiary levels of education. The comparatively high cost of tertiary education, in conjunction with rising levels of donor fatigue, resulted in a considerable decrease in international support for tertiary education in SSA. However, since the turn of the twenty-first century, debate on the relative importance of tertiary education has been informed by an increasing awareness of the sector's importance in knowledge economies and improving international competitiveness. The role of improved access to education and rising levels of educational attainment in driving economic growth is now widely accepted and has been extensively studied. A number of studies have demonstrated the positive relationship between growth in tertiary education and overall economic growth, particularly tertiary education's role in advancing human capital development and technology diffusion (for example, Bloom, Canning, and Chan 2006).

Growing recognition of the critical role played by the tertiary education sector in driving economic development is reflected in the changing composition of education portfolios at the major development banks. A regional case in point is the development of the higher education, science, and technology (HEST) project at the African Development Bank (AfDB), which places a significant emphasis on higher education provision. In 2010, the Asian Development Bank (ADB) published the report *Education by 2020: A Sector Operations Plan* with a close focus on universal secondary education, technical and vocational education, and support for higher education (ADB 2010; Rose and Steer 2013). The share of the total education budget in the official development assistance (ODA) of the

European Union institutions dedicated to tertiary education increased from 27 percent in 2002–04 to 34 percent in 2009–11, whereas the share of the ODA education portfolio dedicated to basic education decreased from 50 to 43 percent over the same period. The share of funds dedicated to tertiary education as a share of the World Bank's total aid envelope for education administered under the auspices of the International Development Association (IDA) increased from 18 percent in 2002–04 to 22 percent in 2009–11 (Rose and Steer 2013).

From the perspective of social justice, society should ensure the fair distribution of public services and equal opportunities for individuals to succeed. Rawls (1971), famous for his idea of "justice as fairness," recognizes that, in order to be just, a society must ensure that all of its members are equally positioned to take advantage of opportunities to access "primary goods"—that is, goods that every rational individual is presumed to want. Although individuals do bear responsibility for their own welfare, their overall level of welfare is also determined by extrinsic factors and conditions over which they have no direct influence. Roemer (1998) argues that equity imperatives demand equal opportunity policies to equalize advantages across disparate groups. Similarly, Dworkin (1981) advocates for a distribution of resources that compensates for external and internal differences (for example, talent) for which individuals cannot be held responsible.

Eliminating inequity in education requires going beyond concepts of social justice and fairness and placing it as an objective alongside other closely linked ones, such as efficiency, sustainability, and relevance. Although the analysis contained in this book emphasizes equity, other equally important factors include the need to improve efficiency in the delivery of tertiary education; the need to sustain the expansion of tertiary education systems in light of rapidly growing demand; and the imperative to improve the relevance of tertiary education in alignment with changing economies. This book argues that efficiency, sustainability, and relevance are of equal importance, and it intends to demonstrate their link with equity: implicit in the analysis contained in this book is the assertion that progress with regard to efficiency, sustainability, and relevance cannot be achieved without improving equity, and vice versa.

Improving equity with regard to educational opportunities helps to improve the efficiency of public service delivery. Most human capital theories argue that individuals invest in education proportionally to their perceived costs and expected returns. However, in imperfect markets, it is difficult for individuals to accurately assess these costs and benefits for optimal planning. When individuals face barriers of access to tertiary education or experience skewed labor market returns to education (as a result of biases relating to gender, class, ethnicity, and the like), they are less inclined to invest in education. In these contexts, the individual and society forgo the benefits associated with the failure to develop this human capital. Very few studies have been conducted on the economic effects of inequity; however, a recent analysis of the effects of Roma exclusion in Eastern Europe quantified the sizable loss in productivity and revenue associated with inequity (World Bank 2010). Equity goals in education should be pursued efficiently—that is, at the lowest possible cost. In some instances, trade-offs may exist with regard to the extent to which efficiency and equity goals can be achieved. In other instances, complementarity (synergy) may exist for pursuing both efficiency and equity. However, countries do not necessarily have to choose between efficiency and equity (Wößmann and Schütz 2006).

Equity contributes to sustainability. Providing free or subsidized tertiary education to students from wealthy families is not only inequitable but also unsustainable in the long run. If participation in higher education is largely "inherited" from one generation to the next, as observed in many SSA countries, it is reflected in the persistent constraint of intergenerational mobility. The 2011 protests in the Arab world, among other things, demonstrated unequivocally that equity in access to tertiary education is an important means for advancing stability and order in society (Salmi and Bassett 2012). Moreover, the "brain drain" caused by many tertiary graduates in SSA leaving their home countries after the completion of their studies not only wastes scarce public resources but is also detrimental to capacity building in these societies.

Expanding tertiary education systems is generally considered in relation to a country's efforts to improve access for underrepresented groups, leading to a shift from elite-dominated systems to more inclusive mass higher education systems. For example, Shavit, Arum, and Gamoran (2007) argue that, when the relative rate of inequality remains stable (but absolute numbers for all groups increase), the fact of expansion itself constitutes a form of inclusion. However, in SSA, the evidence suggests that an increase in the supply of tertiary education does not necessarily translate into greater access for all segments of the population.

Structure of This Book

This book is structured in the following manner:

Chapter 2 discusses the supply and demand of tertiary education in SSA, demonstrating that growth in the demand for tertiary education has far outpaced increased supply. We show that economic development (in terms of gross domestic product [GDP] per capita) is positively associated with tertiary enrollment. Moreover, we demonstrate that the structure of the economy—specifically, the share of the labor force employed in the services and manufacturing sectors—is strongly associated with the number of students benefiting from tertiary education. Chapter 2 also argues that improved access to pretertiary levels of education, and an associated increase in gross enrollment, fuels greater social demand for tertiary education, but that in most instances the improved supply of tertiary education is inadequate to meet increasing demand.

Chapter 3 analyzes key patterns of equity in tertiary education. We demonstrate that, despite rapid growth in tertiary enrollment and improved access for traditionally underserved groups, these energies have not yet transformed SSA tertiary education systems from an elite to a mass system. The relative wealth of the family continues to play a decisive role in an individual's access to tertiary education. Moreover, a child born into a family in which the head of household holds a high school diploma is much more likely to enroll in higher education than a child born into a household in which the head of household has no education. Our analysis demonstrates that regional differences in enrollment are exacerbated by the level of interregional income inequality. Moreover, we show that, although gender parity in tertiary education has improved, biases persist regarding the choice of academic majors for female students. This chapter also highlights the insufficient policy attention extended to students with disabilities.

Chapter 4 focuses on understanding why inequities persist in tertiary education and what factors contribute to the erosion or exacerbation of inequity in tertiary education in SSA. We focus particular attention on inequity in pretertiary levels of education, the effects of skewed public expenditures favoring elites at the tertiary level, opportunity costs implicit in pursuing further education, and the impact of tertiary admissions policies.

Chapter 5 demonstrates that tertiary education yields substantial benefits. The benefits of tertiary education accrue in both market and nonmarket forms for both individuals and society at large. In this chapter we discuss what happens when tertiary students graduate from higher education and attempt to account for disparities in posttertiary outcomes using the following frames of inquiry: (i) private, public, and social returns to tertiary education; and (ii) the impact of tertiary education on social mobility.

Chapter 6 discusses key policy interventions that governments have adopted for the purposes of targeting specific populations to increase access to tertiary education. The effectiveness of interventions in this regard has not been studied extensively, and further research will be required.

Chapter 7 presents country case studies to demonstrate how different tertiary education policies influence outcomes and patterns of equity or inequity.

Key Definitions

Inequality versus Inequity

Inequality and inequity are often used interchangeably, but there are important differences between the two concepts. *Inequality* refers to differences between groups without any consideration of the fairness of those differences, whereas *inequity* presupposes an ethical judgment concerning the differences between groups. In other words, inequity concerns the "process" through which differences arise, and inequality is the "outcome" of this difference.

The Society for International Development (SID 2004) defines inequality as the extent to which the distribution of benefits of economic welfare produced in an economy vary from an equal distribution of these benefits within the population. In the context of education, inequality refers to the extent to which the supply of education as a good, and the benefits that accrue from it, favor certain individuals, groups, generations, races, regions, and so on. According to Barr (2001), equity in the context of tertiary education manifests in a system in which no suitably talented person is denied a place at a university because he or she comes from a disadvantaged background.

Inequality is materially expressed through disparities in constructs of human capital—such as relative poverty, health, education, and economic opportunity—and is often aligned with gender, social class, and race. Inequality in the context of education is usually measured by differences in learning achievement and efficacy (test scores, dropout rates, completion rates, and so on). Inequity refers to unfair situations and conditions that inform unequal outcomes, such as differences in access to education, or access to public subsidies for education, informed by social class, location, gender, and other determining factors. In other words, it is necessary to distinguish between variations in educational outcomes associated with differences in effort and talent and variations in educational outcomes associated with factors beyond an individual's control.

Vertical versus Horizontal Dimensions of Equity

Vertical equity is determined by an analysis of each level of education; the progression of students between cycles of education, such as from secondary to tertiary education; and the completion of tertiary studies. *Horizontal equity* is determined by an analysis of the level of diversification within a tertiary education system and refers to the type of institution or programs attended by socially constructed groups on the basis of factors such as gender and social or economic status as well as with the relative performance of these groups in the labor market (d'Hombres, n.d.).

Enrollment

Enrollment measures the flow of human resources into the education system. The gross enrollment ratio (GER) calculates total enrollment for a specific level of education as a proportion of the total population in the official age group associated with that level of educational development. Because there is no official age group associated with tertiary education and because in many SSA countries a large proportion of students enrolled in tertiary education enter the system many years after the intended age for university entrants, a more effective measure for higher education is to use the number of students enrolled in tertiary education per 100,000 inhabitants. We calculate this number by dividing the total number of students enrolled in tertiary education in a given academic year by the country's total population and multiplying the result by 100,000. Using this measure also enables international comparisons.

Educational Attainment

Educational attainment defines a country's stock of human capital. At the individual level, educational attainment refers to the highest level of education that an individual has achieved (for example, a high school diploma or equivalency certificate, a bachelor's degree, or a master's degree) at a given time, usually measured through a household survey. An example of measuring educational attainment at a collective level is illustrated by the following example: to measure tertiary educational attainment for individuals older than the age of 25 years in Ghana, one would calculate the number of persons age 25 years and above who have attained a tertiary education, divide this number by the total population in this age group, and multiply the result by 100. Mean years of schooling is also used to measure educational attainment in a country. The inequality indicator used in this book, for example, is premised on an analysis of the mean years of schooling for students in the top 20 percent of households by income over mean years of schooling for students drawn from the bottom 80 percent of households.

References

ADB (Asian Development Bank). 2010. *Education by 2020: A Sector Operations Plan*. Manila: ADB.

Barr, N. 2001. *The Welfare State as Piggy Bank: Information, Risk, Uncertainty, and the Role of the State: Information, Risk, Uncertainty, and the Role of the State*. Oxford: Oxford University Press.

Barros, R. D., J. Chanduvi, F. Ferreira, and J. Molinas Vega. 2009. *Measuring Inequality of Opportunities in Latin America and the Caribbean*. Washington, DC: World Bank.

Becker, G. S. 1993. *Human Capital: A Theoretical and Empirical Analysis, with Special Reference to Education*. 3rd ed. Chicago: University of Chicago Press. Orig. pub. 1964.

Bloom, D., D. Canning, and K. Chan. 2006. *Higher Education and Economic Development in Africa*. Washington, DC: World Bank.

Brossard, Mathieu, and Borel Foko. 2008. *Costs and Financing of Higher Education in Francophone Africa*. Washington, DC: World Bank.

Clancy, P., and G. Goastellec. 2007. "Exploring Access and Equity in Higher Education: Policy and Performance in a Comparative Perspective." *Higher Education Quarterly* 61 (2): 136–54.

Devarajan, S., C. L. Monga, and T. Zongo. 2011. "Making Higher Education Finance Work." *Journal of African Economies* 20 (AERC Supplement 3): iii133–54.

d'Hombres, Béatrice. n.d. "Inequality in Tertiary Education Systems: Which Metric Should We Use for Measuring and Benchmarking?" Background Study, World Bank, Washington, DC.

Dworkin, R. 1981. "What Is Equality? Part 2: Equality of Resources." *Philosophy and Public Affairs* 10 (4): 283–345.

Experton, William, and Chloe Fevre. 2010. *Financing Higher Education in Africa*. Directions in Development Series. Washington, DC: World Bank.

Koucky, J., Q. Bartusek, and J. Kovarovic. 2010. *Who Gets a Degree? Access to Tertiary Education in Europe 1959–2009*. Charles University in Prague, Faculty of Education.

Mincer, J. 1974. *Schooling, Experience, and Earnings*. New York: National Bureau of Economic Research.

Ogawa, K., and K. Iimura. 2010. "Determinants of Access and Equity in Tertiary Education: The Case of Indonesia." *Excellence in Higher Education* 1 (1&2): 3–22.

Rawls, J. 1971. *A Theory of Justice*. Cambridge, MA: Harvard University Press.

Roemer, J. E. 1998. *Theories of Distributive Justice*. Cambridge, MA: Harvard University Press.

Rose, P., and L. Steer. 2013. *Financing for Global Education: Opportunities for Multilateral Action*. Washington and New York: Brookings Institution and United Nations Educational, Scientific, and Cultural Organization.

Salmi, J., and R. M. Bassett. 2012. "Opportunities for All? The Equity Challenge in Tertiary Education." Salzburg Global Seminar, Salzburg, Austria.

Salmi, J., B. Millot, D. Court, M. Crawford, P. Darvas, F. Golladay, L. Holm-Nielsen, R. Hopper, A. Markov, P. Moock, H. Mukherjee, W. Saint, S. Shrivastava, F. Steier, and R. van Meel. 2002. *Constructing Knowledge Societies*. Directions in Development Series. Washington, DC: World Bank.

Schultz, T. W. 1961. "Investment in Human Capital." *American Economic Review* 51 (1): 1–17.

Shavit, Yossi, Richard Arum, and Adam Gamoran, eds. 2007. *Stratification in Higher Education: A Comparative Study*. Social Inequality Series. Stanford, CA: Stanford University Press.

SID (Society for International Development). 2004. *Pulling Apart: Facts and Figures on Inequality in Kenya*. Nairobi: SID.

Thomas, V., Y. Wang, and X. Fan. 2001. "Measuring Education Inequality: Gini Coefficients of Education." Policy Research Working Paper 2525, World Bank, Washington, DC.

Varghese, N. V. 2004. *Private Higher Education in Africa*. Paris: International Institute for Education Planning (IIEP) and United Nations Educational, Scientific, and Cultural Organization (UNESCO).

Walenkamp, J., and A. Boeren. 2007. "What Donors Should Do." *Development & Cooperation*, No. 9.

World Bank. 2009. *Accelerating Catch-Up: Tertiary Education for Growth in Sub-Saharan Africa*. Directions in Development Series. Washington, DC: World Bank.

———. 2010. *Economic Cost of Roma Exclusion*. Washington, DC: World Bank.

Wößmann, L., and G. Schütz. 2006. *Efficiency and Equity in European Education and Training Systems*. Brussels: European Commission.

Zhang, J., and T. Li. 2002. "International Inequality and Convergence in EducationalAttainment, 1960–1990." *Review of Development Economics* 6: 383–92.

CHAPTER 2

Supply and Demand

Key Messages

- Growth in supply of tertiary education in Sub-Saharan Africa (SSA) has been phenomenal; however, it is still outstripped by growth in the demand for tertiary education.
- Diversification has played a key role in the expansion of supply in tertiary education in SSA, including both horizontal and vertical diversification.
- Development of tertiary education has been positively associated with economic development and upgrading of the economy (measured by the share of the labor force working in the services and manufacturing sectors).
- Absolute and relative enrollment growth in pre-tertiary cycles of education has fueled increased social demand for tertiary education, but the supply of tertiary education is inadequate to absorb the increasing number of senior secondary graduates.

Growth in Supply

Although SSA has witnessed exponential growth in enrollment in tertiary education, the region still continues to demonstrate the lowest participation rate in tertiary education in the world. In 2013, there were 7.2 million students enrolled in tertiary education in SSA, compared with fewer than 400,000 students in 1970. The gross enrollment ratio (GER) for tertiary education grew at an average annual rate of 4.3 percent between 1970 and 2013, compared with a global annual average increase of 2.8 percent over the same period (figure 2.1).

However, growth in enrollment is still insufficient to meet rising demand for tertiary education, and the pressure on SSA countries to further expand access to tertiary education is increasing. This pressure is driven by factors including economic growth, "demographic dividend," improved enrollment in primary and secondary education, and structural shifts in the economy away from primary sector activities and toward the manufacturing and services sectors.

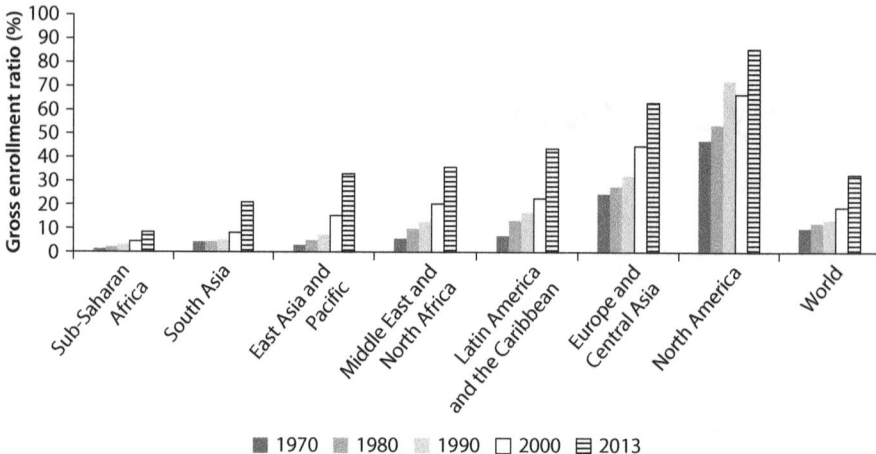

Figure 2.1 Gross Enrollment Ratio, by Region, 1970–2013

Source: Calculations are based on UIS data.

Diversification of Supply

Diversification is the process in which nontraditional types of tertiary education emerge in response to demand for educational programs that (i) equip students with skills and knowledge aligned with shifting demand within the economy and (ii) cater to a wider range of students with different needs and abilities. Within tertiary education systems, *vertical diversification* occurs when distinct types of institutions appear in response to labor market demand, complementing traditional research universities in the form of polytechnics, professional institutes, nonresearch universities, and junior colleges. *Horizontal diversification* also takes place as new types of educational providers—for-profit, nonprofit, religious, international, and local government entities—emerge to fulfill unmet demand (Ng'ethe, Subotzky, and Afeti 2008).

Horizontal Diversification

Although the development of private higher education in SSA is a relatively recent phenomenon, emerging in most countries in the late 1980s, this subsector of tertiary education has demonstrated spectacular growth over the past two and a half decades. Between 1990 and 2014, the number of public universities in the region increased from an estimated 100 to 500. In comparison, the number of private tertiary institutions increased from approximately 30 in 1990 to over 1,000 in 2014 (Bloom et al. 2014). In some countries—including Chad, Côte d'Ivoire, the Republic of Congo, and Uganda—the share of enrollment in private higher education institutions has tripled or quadrupled over the last decade (figure 2.2).

According to Varghese (2004) five primary factors account for the rapid expansion of private tertiary education institutions in SSA: (i) the inability of the public sector to meet growing social demand for tertiary education;

Figure 2.2 Share of Tertiary Enrollment in Private Institutions, 2000 and 2012

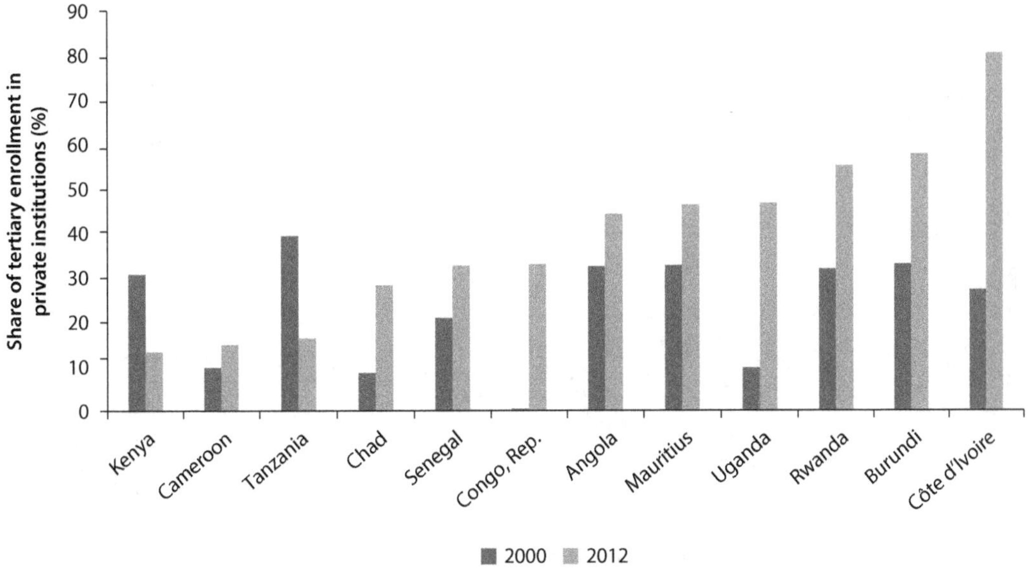

Source: Calculations are based on UIS data.
Note: UIS = United Nations Educational, Scientific, and Cultural Organization Institute for Statistics.

(ii) declining subsidies to the social sector; (iii) demand for programs and courses more appropriately aligned with the needs of the labor market; (iv) the perception that operations in the private sector are comparatively more efficient than those of the public sector; and (v) the privatization of public universities in line with broader economic policy shifts away from state planning, and toward market forces.

The development of private higher education depends on state policies, resulting in different development paths across the countries of the region. Figure 2.3 illustrates the proportion of private tertiary enrollment as a share of total tertiary enrollment (per 100,000 inhabitants). It demonstrates that, in a majority of countries with relatively low numbers of students enrolled in higher education per 100,000 residents, a relatively small share of students are enrolled in the private higher education subsector (for example, Burkina Faso and Zimbabwe). At the other end of the spectrum, while more than 80 percent of tertiary enrollment in Côte d'Ivoire is accounted for by private institutions, the number of tertiary students per 100,000 inhabitants is less than 500. Examples of outlier tertiary systems may illustrate lessons for, and challenges to, countries seeking to expand private tertiary education provision.

Vertical Diversification

As the labor market increasingly demands readily employable graduates ("finished products"), demand for education shifts away from traditional, more theoretical higher education programs and toward occupation-related programs

Figure 2.3 Number of Tertiary Students per 100,000 Inhabitants versus Share of Students Enrolled in Private Higher Education, 2012

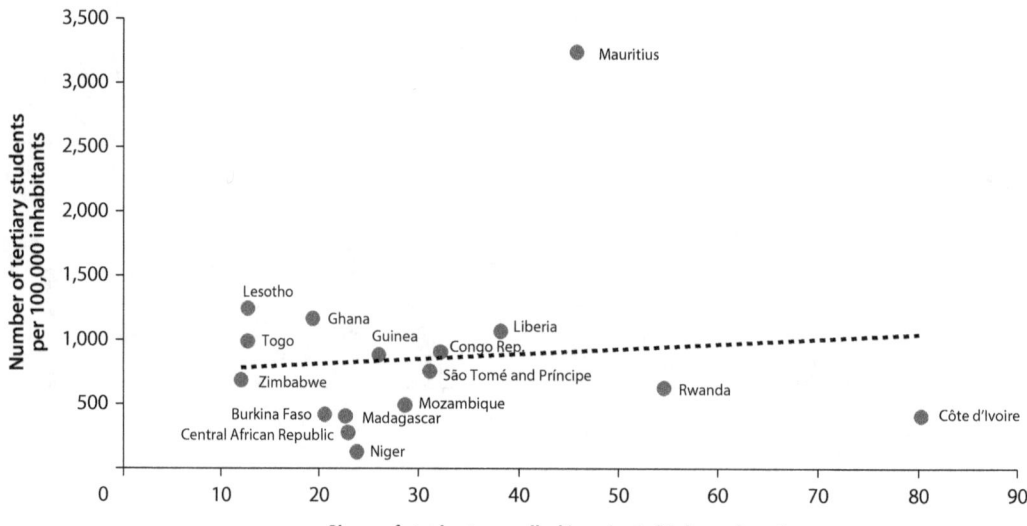

Source: Calculations are based on UIS data.
Note: UIS = United Nations Educational, Scientific, and Cultural Organization Institute for Statistics.

of study that are perceived to produce a more vocationally trained labor force (Varghese 2004). The rise of nonuniversity institutions for tertiary education, such as polytechnics and institutions catering to short-cycle programs of study, is a response to this shifting demand. In 10 of 19 SSA countries for which data were available, short-cycle technical/vocational courses accounted for more than a quarter of tertiary enrollment in 2012 (figure 2.4).

The traditional dichotomy between universities and nonuniversity tertiary institutions and education has also become increasingly blurred. In some instances, interesting university/nonuniversity institutional hybrids have emerged, for example, the Kigali Institute of Science, Technology and Management (KIST) in Rwanda, so-called Comprehensive Universities in South Africa, and the University of Malawi. In general, there is a lack of policy clarity in SSA systems of tertiary education regarding appropriate boundaries between polytechnics and universities in terms of their mission, purpose, curricula, and programs (Ng'ethe, Subotzky, and Afeti 2008).

In developed countries where diversification of the tertiary education landscape occurred more intensively, the higher education GERs doubled (or in some cases tripled) between the 1980s and 1990s (Varghese 2004). However, the strength of correlation between increasing nonuniversity enrollment and overall enrollment in tertiary education in SSA is not clear. In some SSA countries an increasing share of nonuniversity sector enrollment has not translated into increasing overall enrollment rates (figure 2.5). Côte d'Ivoire, for example, demonstrates low overall tertiary enrollment and high short-cycle enrollment.

Supply and Demand

Figure 2.4 Share of Short-Cycle Tertiary Education in Total Tertiary Education, 2012

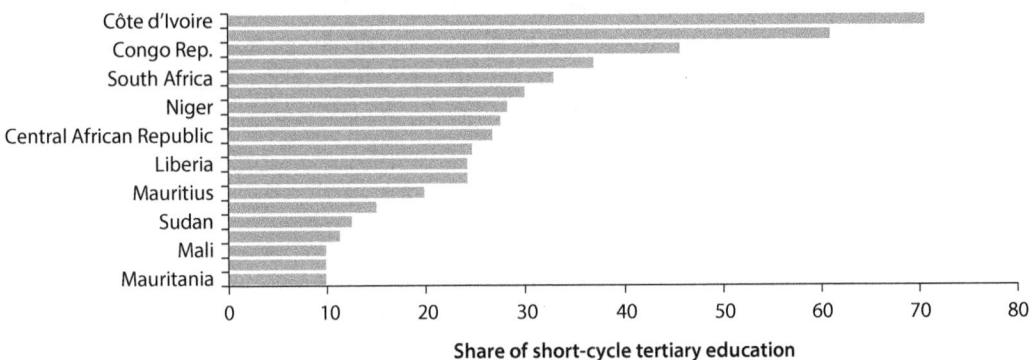

Source: World Bank EdStats.

Figure 2.5 Enrollment in Short-Cycle Tertiary Education versus Overall Tertiary Enrollment

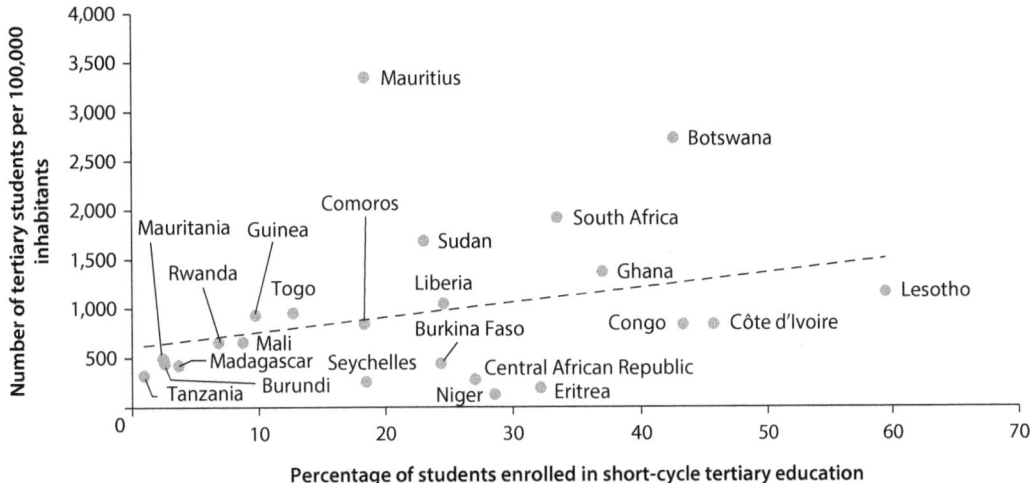

Source: Calculations are based on UIS data.
Note: Data are from 2013 or the latest year for which data are available. UIS = United Nations Educational, Scientific, and Cultural Organization Institute for Statistics.

In Mauritius, the opposite trajectory is evident: high tertiary enrollment and a relatively low share of enrollment in short-cycle tertiary education. South Africa demonstrates relatively high tertiary enrollment and a high share of short-cycle educational enrollment as a share of total enrollment.

Demand and Economic Development

Over the course of the past decade, most countries in SSA have experienced sustained and strong economic growth. In 2014, 4 of the 10 fastest-growing economies in the world, measured in terms of annual GDP growth, were in the SSA region.

Contemporary growth has been underpinned by improved macroeconomic stability, implementation of reforms to address market failure and inefficient markets, a reduction in trade barriers, and, most consequentially, a rapid increase in demand for natural resource–based commodities (World Bank 2009). However, a continued disproportionate dependence on commodity exports exposes resource-rich economies in SSA to shocks associated with volatility in commodity prices. The recent slowdown in the Chinese economy, the tapering of global demand for commodities, and the exponential fall in the global price of oil have had a significant and negative effect on African economic performance in the short term. Economic output recovered to 4 percent across the region in 2015. Although this is below the historic average of 4.4 percent, it is still above the projection for global economic growth of 2.9 percent in 2015. In 2016 the collective economic growth of SSA was projected to gradually increase to 4.5 percent (World Bank 2015).

Improved economic performance is positively associated with the expansion of tertiary education, as shown in figure 2.6. From the supply side, this is a result of governments being in an improved position to finance subsidies for the sector; from the demand side, the demand for nontraditional tertiary education increases, such as short-cycle universities that focus on specific skills that are considered to be highly relevant in the labor market.

At the household level, the correlation between income and schooling is not strong.[1] The outcome of schooling depends on a range of factors. These include

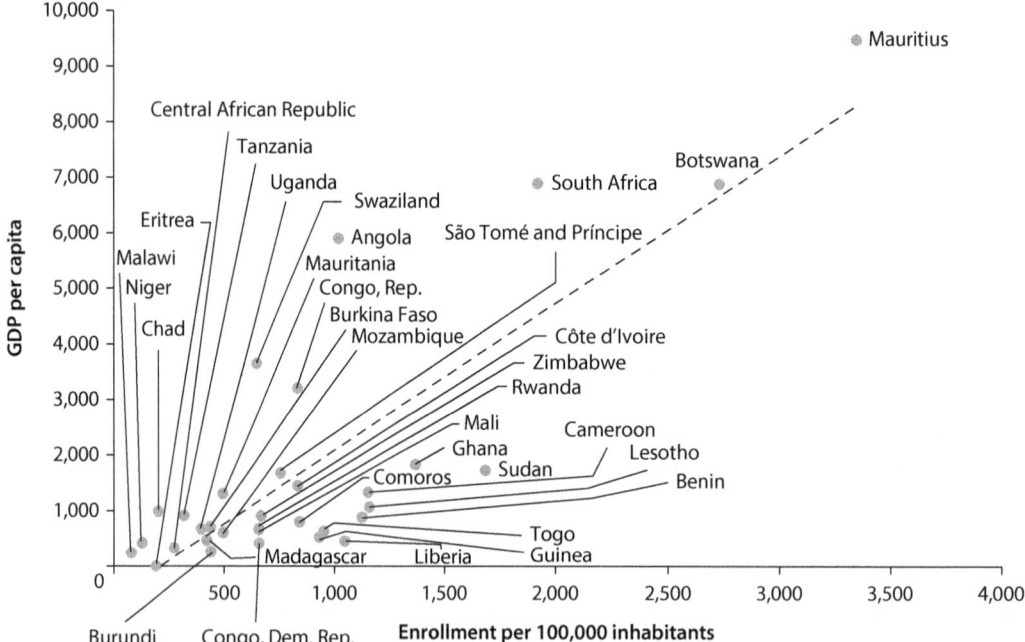

Figure 2.6 Tertiary Enrollment per 100,000 Inhabitants and GDP per Capita (Current US$), 2013

Source: Calculations are based on UIS data.

access to pre-tertiary education, improved literacy (of parents as well as students), gender, location, better information on the benefits of education and its opportunity costs, and the existence of more and better jobs for tertiary graduates. Analyses of lower levels of education demonstrate a weak correlation between household income and educational attainment. In Côte d'Ivoire, for example, research demonstrates that households in urban areas that own and operate their own (nonagricultural) enterprises are less likely to send their children to school. In this particular context, it may be that a child's present-day contribution to the enterprise is perceived as being more valuable than the perceived returns to further education (Bredie and Beeharry 1998).

The effects of improved household economic status on educational attainment manifest over a long period of time. After those in the first generation rise out of poverty, they may send their children to school. Depending on a student's record of attendance and performance, a household may support enrollment in higher levels of schooling. For a family, this could play out over 15–20 years, meaning that effective and comprehensive poverty alleviation measures could lead to higher demand for tertiary education in 15–20 years.

Economic Structure and Diversification

Notwithstanding significant variance across countries, the agricultural sector in SSA continues to employ half of the labor force and contributes approximately one-fifth of regional gross domestic product (GDP). Data from the most recent household surveys (the Living Standard Measurement Study, or LSMS) demonstrate that the share of agricultural employment as a proportion of total employment ranges from 83 percent in Malawi to less than 20 percent in Mauritania (figure 2.7).

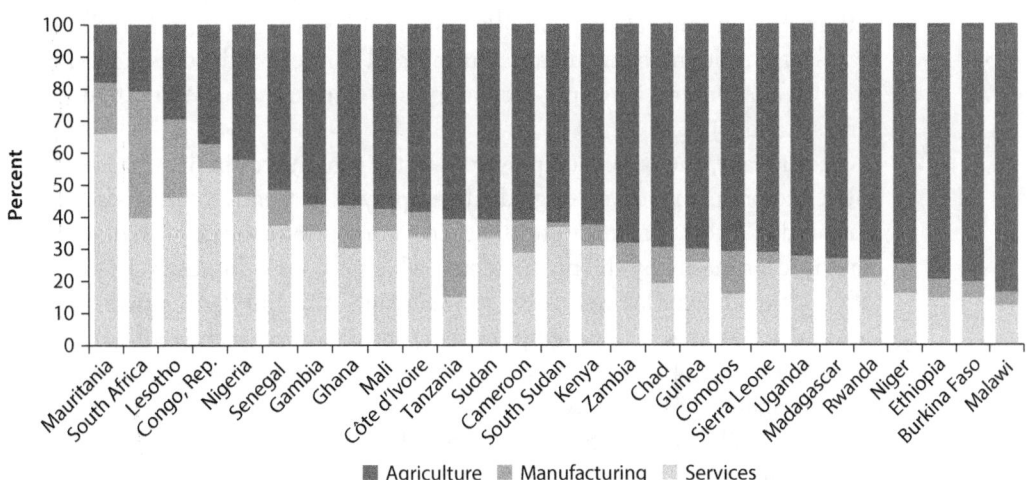

Figure 2.7 Economic Structure by Employment, Latest Household Survey

Source: Calculations are based on LSMS data.

Empirical evidence from other regions suggests that rapid productivity growth driven by more intensive use of skilled labor and technology is usually associated with a declining share of agriculture to GDP (and the share of employment accounted for by this sector). In Ghana, for example, drawing on data from the Population and Housing Census (PHC), the share of agricultural employment as a share of total employment declined from 53.1 percent in 2000 to 41.6 percent in 2010. This decline was accompanied by an increase in the share of employment associated with the services sector, which increased from 31.4 percent to 43.2 percent over the same period. The share of employment associated with the industrial sector, however, remained relatively constant (Hino and Ranis 2014).

Although a significant proportion of SSA's labor force will continue to find work in the agriculture sector, employment trends are shifting. In general, the services sector has been more successful in stimulating output, exports, and labor productivity than the manufacturing sector. Because growth over the course of the past decade has been disproportionately concentrated in the services sector, the International Monetary Fund (IMF 2012) has projected that contemporary workers and future entrants to the labor force will disproportionately seek employment in the services sector.

Economic growth in SSA is characterized by an overdependence on a limited number of export-oriented and labor-intensive industries. From a comparative perspective, the services sector is in a nascent phase of development, with the majority of activity undertaken by small and medium-sized enterprises located in the informal economy. In general, the business environment is characterized by weak or absent regulatory frameworks, poor infrastructure, expensive licensing requirements, informational asymmetries, unfair recruitment practices, clientelism, and low levels of productivity (Montanini 2013).

Against this backdrop, the increasing share of employment attributed to the manufacturing and services sectors demonstrates increasing economic diversification. However, the increasing share of employment in these sectors is not necessarily associated with increasing penetration, and use, of technology or with improved innovation. Notwithstanding this caveat, countries with higher shares of employment in manufacturing and services industries have higher rates of enrollment in upper-secondary and tertiary education (figure 2.8, panels a and b).

Traditionally, the largest employer of tertiary graduates in SSA has been the public sector. In an analysis of graduate employment trends in SSA, Mingat and Majgaard (2008) demonstrate that secondary and tertiary graduates are employed primarily by the public sector, which accounts for just 4.1 percent of total regional employment. By comparison, the modern private sector (5.4 percent of total regional employment) absorbs fewer highly skilled workers; 16 percent of employees in the public sector are graduates from tertiary institutions, compared with 8 percent in the modern private sector.

Figure 2.9 illustrates substantial country-level variance in the share of tertiary graduates in public sector employment. Public sector workforces in the countries located on the right side of the graph—for example, Ghana and Sierra Leone—are

Figure 2.8 Share of Manufacturing and Services Employment

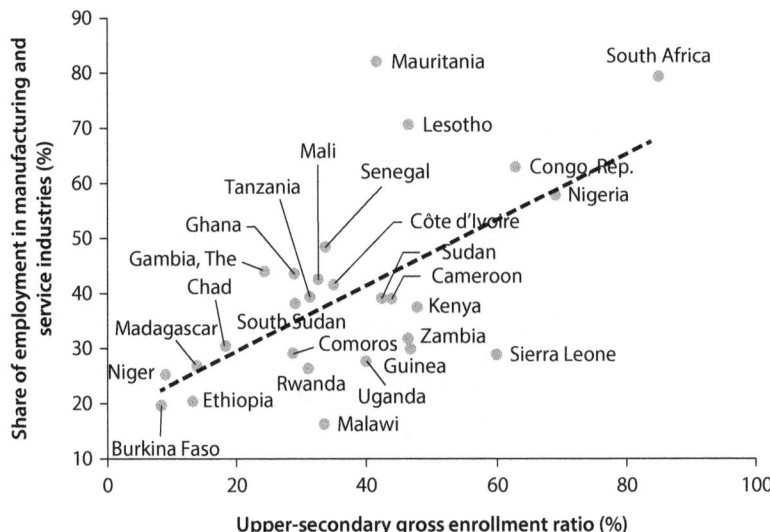

a. Share of manufacturing and services employment and upper-secondary GER

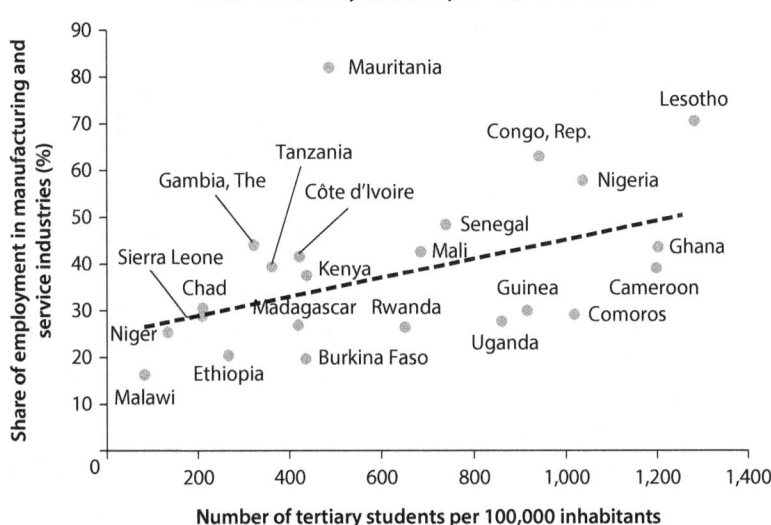

b. Share of manufacturing and services employment with number of tertiary students per 100,000 inhabitants

Sources: Calculations are based on LSMS data and UIS data.
Note: LSMS = ; UIS = United Nations Educational, Scientific, and Cultural Organization Institute for Statistics.

characterized by a large share of employees holding tertiary qualifications, despite the fact that the tertiary sectors in Ghana and Sierra Leone are at very different stages of development. Countries on the left side of the graph—for example, Kenya and Burkina Faso—demonstrate significantly lower shares of employees with tertiary qualifications.

Figure 2.9 Tertiary GER and the Share of Employees with Tertiary Education in the Public Sector

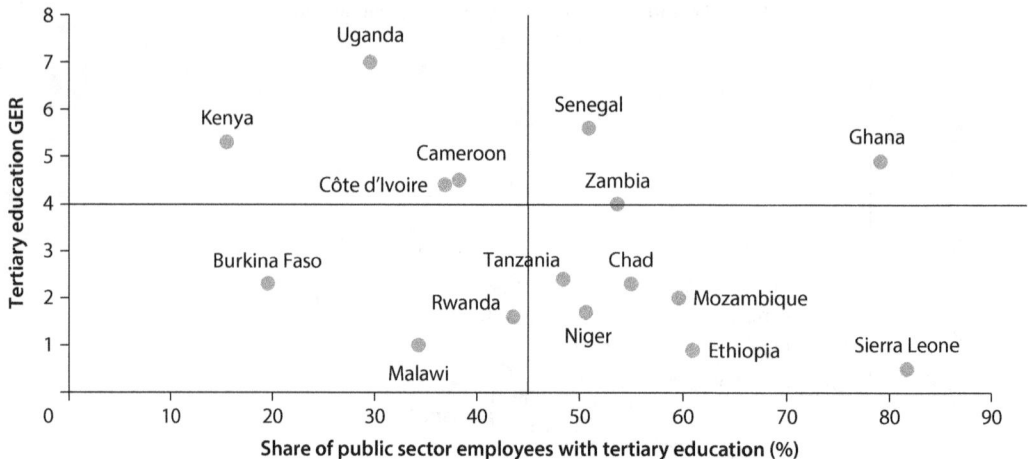

Source: Calculations are based on LSMS data.
Note: GER = gross enrollment ratio; LSMS = Living Standards Measurement Study.

Public sector employment does not provide the right incentives for skills. Savoie and Brecher (1992) point out that public sector jobs in SSA generally link salary scales to educational qualifications. Promotion is generally associated with age seniority and is processed almost automatically with little reference to performance. Public service employment is often characterized by an absence of well-defined job descriptions and an absence of evaluation criteria; and, in many instances, continued employment is guaranteed by tenure. Finally, monetary compensation is often supplemented with generous fringe benefits.

Because of the nature of the civil service, public sector employment does not grow quickly, and the private sector may therefore be considered the primary driver for increased demand for skills associated with tertiary education. In 2011, approximately 50 percent of higher education graduates were employed by the public sector in SSA, a decline from approximately 60 percent in 1999 (Hino and Ranis 2014).

In general, SSA labor markets lack an effective mechanism for evaluating the skill and merit of graduates, contributing to the skills mismatch in the labor market. In Cameroon, Côte d'Ivoire, Madagascar, Mauritania, Niger, Nigeria, Senegal, Tanzania, and Uganda, tertiary graduates have higher unemployment rates than youth with only a primary or secondary education (Amelewonu and Brossard 2005). In Kenya it takes, on average, five years for a university graduate to find employment (Omolo 2010). Moreover, Mingat and Majgaard (2008) have noted that eight of the nine countries characterized by high graduate unemployment are Francophone, which is likely a consequence of the particularities of their admission policies (discussed in more detail in chapter 6).

The tertiary education sector in SSA has traditionally played a weak role in the diffusion of technology and innovation, or the promotion of entrepreneurship.

Universities in developing countries often function at the periphery of the international scientific community, unable to participate in the production and adaptation of knowledge to successfully address domestic economic and social problems (Salmi et al. 2002). Curricula design and course offerings, in many contexts, are not based on local conditions or the particularities of the domestic labor market. These conditions contribute to a situation in which higher education does not necessarily equip individuals with skills for self-advancement, and graduates emerge from the tertiary sector without the skills demanded by, or in alignment with the needs of, the labor market.

To remedy this situation, there must be greater willingness on the part of governments to pursue further economic diversification and the development of job-creating industries, and universities must more effectively fulfill their intended role of servicing the economy through research and knowledge development. Public investment to facilitate improved power generation, infrastructure development, and the implementation of macroeconomic policies to give the private sector access to finance can have long-lasting effects for improving the business environment. Institutions of higher learning can more effectively support the development of a competitive private sector, and supply firms with the skilled workers they demand, by revising curricula to better align programs with the needs of the economy and by increasing collaboration with the private sector (Hino and Ranis 2014).

Growth in Pre-Tertiary Enrollment

SSA is experiencing a "demographic dividend." With 200 million residents between 15 and 24 years of age, Africa has the youngest population in the world. Moreover, the absolute number of residents in this generational cohort is expected to double by 2045. In 2012, 42 percent of 20–24 year olds in the region completed a full cycle of secondary education. As a consequence of significant progress toward the achievement of universal primary education, the share of 20–24 year olds in the region who have completed a full cycle of secondary education is projected to rise to 59 percent by 2030, equivalent to 137 million people (AfDB et al. 2012).

Pre-tertiary education has grown rapidly in SSA. For example, between 2000 and 2012, enrollment in upper-secondary education grew most rapidly in the East Asia and Pacific region (4.5 percent annualized growth), followed by South Asia (3.9 percent) and SSA (3.5 percent) (figure 2.10).

Despite improved enrollment in lower cycles of education, poor transition rates between secondary school and tertiary education persist. The abysmal rate of transition to tertiary education is a result of a range of factors, including low completion rates in secondary education, the perception that further educational attainment is not necessarily associated with higher earnings (Salmi et al. 2002), and the persistence of elitist practices in African university systems. In 2013, the GER for tertiary education in SSA was 8.5 percent, about a quarter of the GER for upper-secondary education, at 34.8 percent. Globally, the GER for tertiary education is approximately half that of secondary education.

Figure 2.10 Upper-Secondary Education GER and Growth Rate, 2000 and 2012

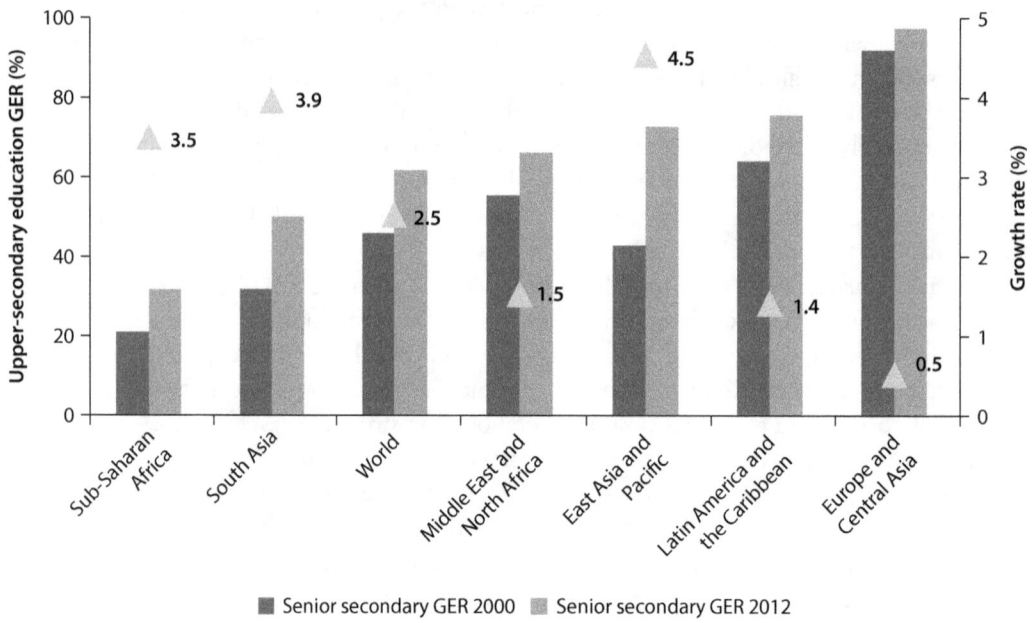

Source: Calculations are based on UIS data.
Note: GER = gross enrollment ratio; UIS = United Nations Educational, Scientific, and Cultural Organization Institute for Statistics.

Figure 2.11 Senior Secondary and Tertiary GER

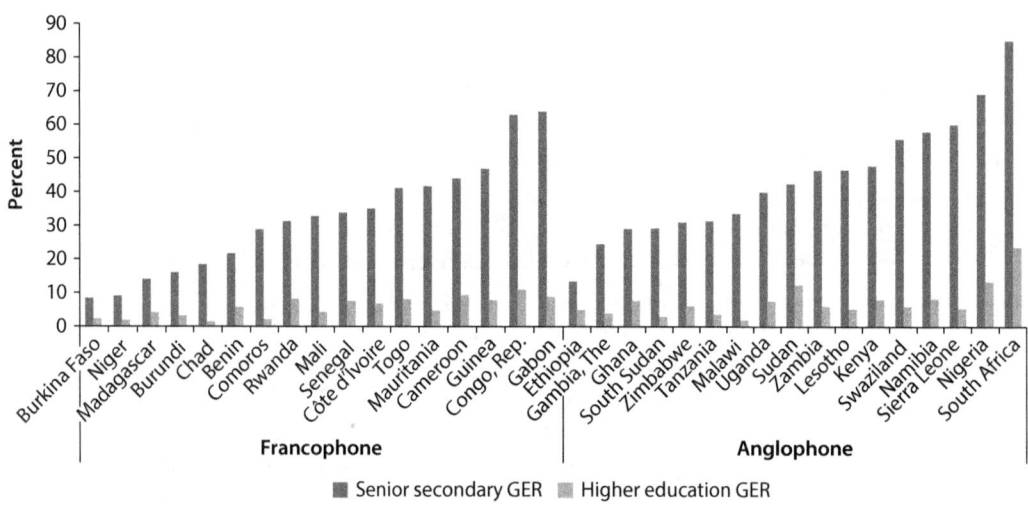

Source: Calculations are based on latest household surveys.
Note: GER = gross enrollment ratio.

Francophone and Anglophone countries demonstrate distinct profiles in terms of upper-secondary enrollment (figure 2.11). The average GER for upper-secondary education in Anglophone countries is higher than that observed in the Francophone countries of the region. This may be a result of the improved capacity of Anglophone education systems to absorb over-aged students and the higher levels of gender disparity in terms of enrollment in most Francophane countries as compared with their Anglophone neighbors (Lewin and Sabates 2011).

Note

1. The term "schooling" used here colloquially refers to educational attainment as described in chapter 1.

References

AfDB, OECD, UNDP, and UNECA (African Development Bank, Organisation for Economic Co-operation and Development, United Nations Development Programme, and United Nations Economic Commission for Africa). 2012. *African Economic Outlook: Promoting Youth Employment*. Paris: OECD Publishing.

Amelewonu, K., and M. Brossard. 2005. *Développer l'éducation Secondaire en Afrique: Enjeux, contraintes et marges de manœuvre*. Addis Ababa: UNESCO–BREDA.

Bloom, D. E., D. Canning, K. Chan, and D. L. Luca. 2014. "Higher Education and Economic Growth in Africa." *International Journal of African Higher Education* 1 (1): 22–57.

Bredie, J. W., and G. K. Beeharry. 1998. "School Enrollment Decline in Sub-Saharan Africa." World Bank Discussion Paper 395, World Bank, Washington, DC.

Hino, H., and G. Ranis. 2014. *Youth and Employment in Sub-Saharan Africa: Working but Poor*. New York: Routledge.

IMF (International Monetary Fund). 2012. *World Economic and Financial Surveys, Regional Economic Outlook, Sub-Saharan Africa*. Washington, DC: IMF.

Lewin, K., and R. Sabates. 2011. *Changing Patterns of Access to Education in Anglophone and Francophone Countries in Sub Saharan Africa: Is Education for All Pro-Poor?* Research Monograph No. 52, CREATE.

Mingat, A., and K. Majgaard. 2008. *A Cross-Country Study of Education in Sub-Saharan Africa*. Washington, DC: World Bank.

Montanini, M. 2013. "Supporting Tertiary Education, Enhancing Economic Development." ISPI Working Paper 49, Istituto per gli Studi di Politica Internazionale, Milan.

Ng'ethe, N., Subotzky, G., and Afeti, G. 2008. *Differentiation and Articulation in Tertiary Education Systems: A Study of Twelve African Countries*. Washington, DC: World Bank.

Omolo, O. 2010. *The Dynamics and Trends of Employment in Kenya*. IEA Research Paper Series. Nairobi: Institute of Economic Affairs.

Salmi, J., B. Millot, D. Court, M. Crawford, P. Darvas, F. Golladay, L. Holm-Nielsen, R. Hopper, A. Markov, P. Moock, H. Mukherjee, W. Saint, S. Shrivastava, F. Steier, and R. van Meel. 2002. *Constructing Knowledge Societies*. Directions in Development Series. Washington, DC: World Bank.

Savoie, D. J., and I. Brecher. 1992. *Equity and Efficiency in Economic Development: Essays in Honour of Benjamin Higgins*. Montreal: McGill–Queen's University Press.

UIS (UNESCO Institute for Statistics). 2012. *Reaching Out-of-School Children Is Crucial for Development*. Paris: United Nations Educational, Scientific, and Cultural Organization.

Varghese, N. V. 2004. *Private Higher Education in Africa*. Paris: International Institute for Education Planning (IIEP) and Paris: United Nations Educational, Scientific, and Cultural Organization.

World Bank. 2009. *Accelerating Catch-Up: Tertiary Education for Growth in Sub-Saharan Africa*. Directions in Development Series. Washington, DC: World Bank.

———. 2015. *Africa's Pulse*. Washington, DC: World Bank.

CHAPTER 3

Equity Patterns

Key Messages

- Despite significant growth in tertiary employment and an increase in the provision of higher education to traditionally underserved groups, systems of tertiary education in Sub-Saharan Africa (SSA) have not yet transformed themselves from elite to mass systems of education.
- Relative household wealth continues to play a decisive role in informing the likelihood that an individual successfully accesses tertiary education.
- Children born into households in which the head of household has completed secondary education are far more likely to attend university than are children born into households whose head has no education.
- Although gender parity in tertiary education has improved, discrimination regarding the choice of majors for female students persists.
- Regional differences are intertwined with gaps in economic development.
- In general, systems of tertiary education in SSA have not paid sufficient policy attention to the needs of students with disabilities.

Socioeconomic Status

The gap between the rich and poor in SSA is a significant social issue. In Kenya, for example, the top 1 percent of income earners make on average $1,204 a month, whereas the highest wage accruing to the bottom 90 percent of income earners is approximately $181 a month (Mulongo 2013). South Africa, the most developed country on the continent, demonstrates the highest disparity in income distribution (figure 3.1).

In many SSA countries, students from households in the highest income quintiles dominate enrollment in universities and other institutions of higher education (figure 3.2). In general, the participation of students from households in lower quintiles of income is higher in comparatively wealthy countries. Moreover, Anglophone countries demonstrate fewer disparities than Francophone countries, and, from a geographic perspective, countries in East and West Africa

Figure 3.1 Distribution of Income or Consumption, by Quintile

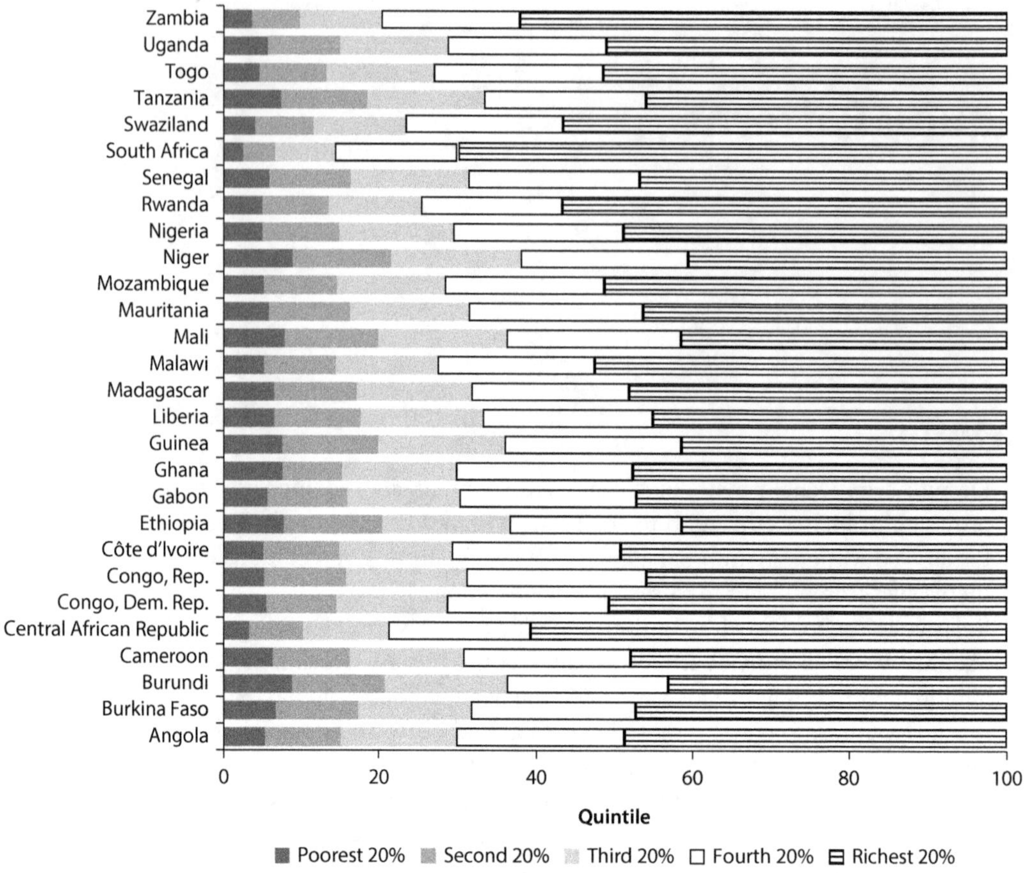

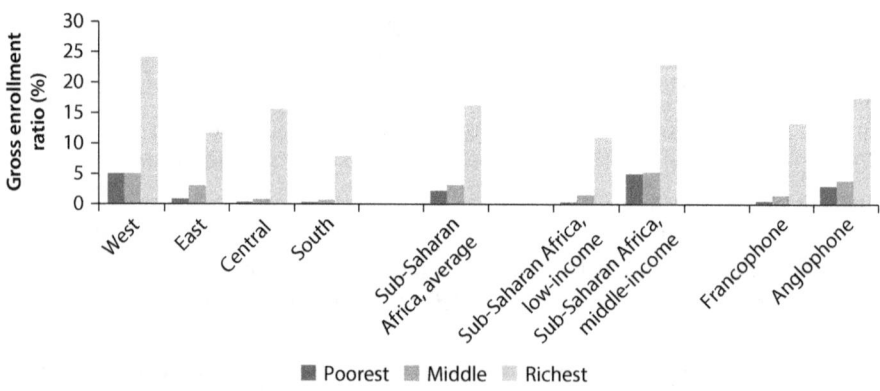

Source: Calculations are based on LSMS data.

Figure 3.2 Tertiary Education GER by Wealth Quintiles, by Sub-Saharan African Region

Source: Calculations are based on LSMS data.
Note: GER = gross enrollment ratio.

Equity Patterns

demonstrate relatively higher levels of equity than their peers in South and Central Africa.

The gross enrollment ratio (GER) for low-income students in postsecondary education is growing at a slower rate than that for the students from the highest 20 percent of households by income. In countries for which data are available, postsecondary enrollment for students from the bottom 80 percent of households by income increased by approximately 3.1 percent between 1998 and 2012 (3.5 percent for Anglophone countries, and 2.4 percent for Francophone countries), compared with an increase of 7.9 percent for students from the highest 20 percent of households (7.2 percent for Anglophone countries, and 9.4 percent for Francophone countries). As the data cited in parentheses above demonstrate, it is evident that GER disparity is lower in Anglophone countries than in Francophone countries when observing students from different income backgrounds. (figure 3.3, panels a and b).

Figure 3.3 Gross Enrollment Ratio for Postsecondary Education for African Countries

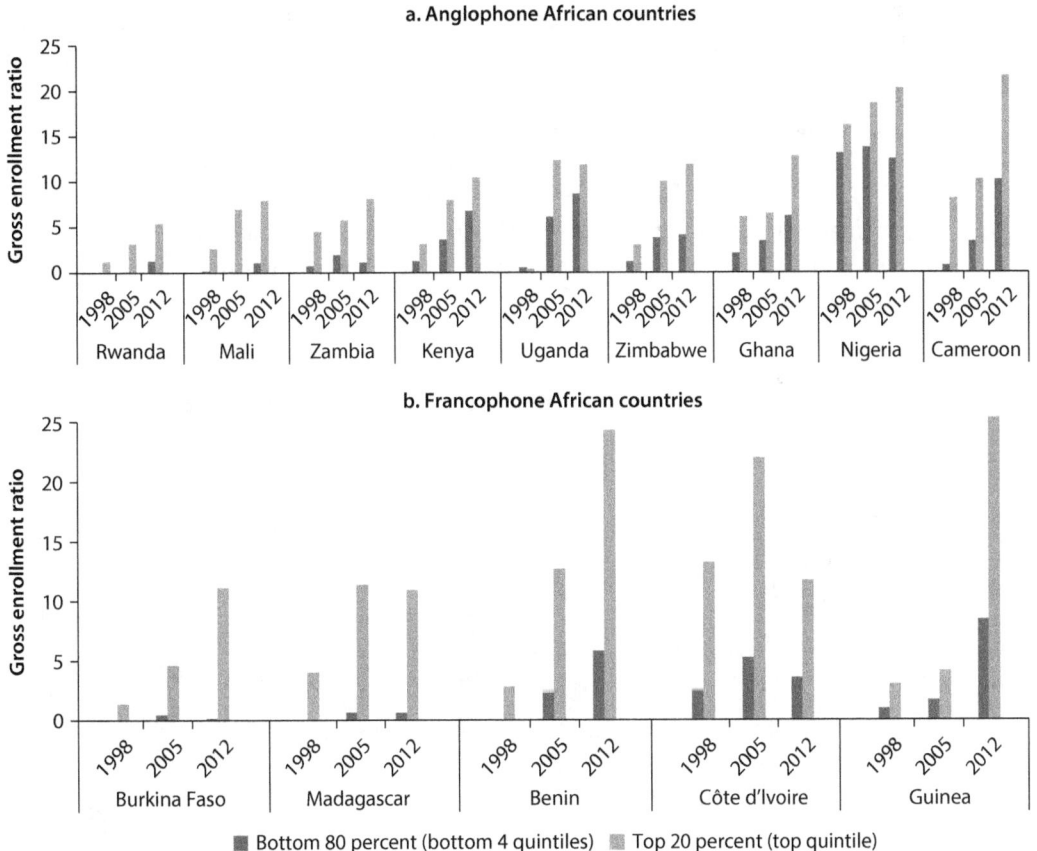

Source: Calculations are based on UIS data from DHS.
Note: Secondary gross attendance rate is the number of postsecondary school pupils of any age, expressed as a percentage of youth of postsecondary school age. Postsecondary school age is defined as the age range from graduation from secondary school till the maximum age set as a parameter of the educational system. UIS = United Nations Educational, Scientific, and Cultural Organization Institute for Statistics.

Beyond the matter of enrollment and attendance, students from disadvantaged backgrounds who do enroll in higher education are more likely to drop out than their peers from comparatively privileged backgrounds. Because of a higher incidence of interrupting studies for periods of full-time employment, lower-income students are also more likely to take longer to complete their education than students from richer households (Chimanikire 2009).

Gender

Many of the positive social implications associated with education are linked to increased participation on the part of female students. As a consequence, female education is disproportionately important for improved social welfare. However, across SSA, gender-based disparities persist in tertiary enrollment. In SSA as a whole, the GER for the female population increased from 3.7 percent in 2000 to 7.0 percent in 2013, at an annual rate of increase of 5 percent. Despite this significant progress, for every 100 male students enrolled in the tertiary education systems of SSA in 2013, there were only approximately 72 female students. Gender inequity is further underlined by important differences in the GER for male and female students, at 9.9 percent and 7 percent, respectively. Moreover, growth in the female GER for tertiary education in SSA has been at a slower rate than the international average of 6 percent—surpassing the growth in female enrollment only in the Arab states (4 percent) and Eastern Europe and Central Asia (3 percent). This is unremarkable because both regions have higher rates of female enrollment to begin with (figure 3.4). Last, SSA and South Asia are the only regions where men increasingly outnumber women in tertiary education participation.

Figure 3.4 Gross Enrollment Ratio, Gender Parity Index, and Tertiary Education

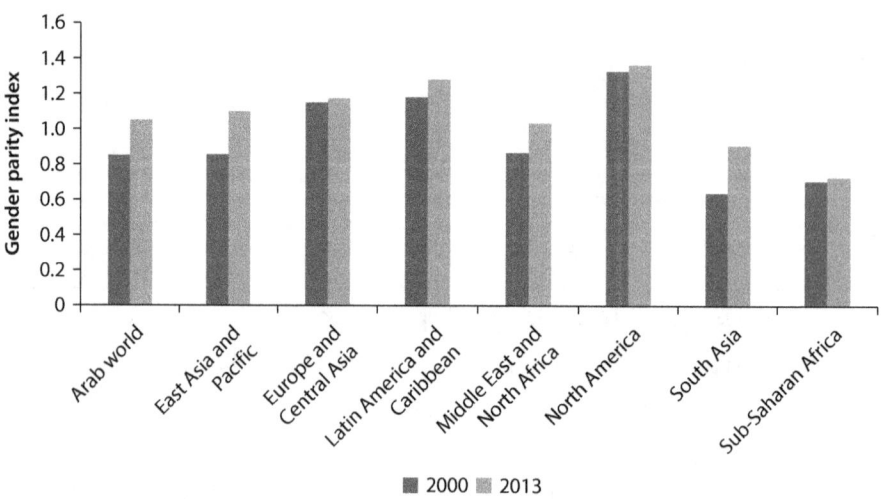

Source: World Bank EdStats 2015.

Equity Patterns

The legacy of colonialism accounts in part for the persistence of gender inequity in tertiary education. Colonial educational systems were established for the purpose of exclusively educating African men to serve in subordinate support and clerical positions (Egbo 2000). To this day, the entrenched gender biases and unintentionally gender-insensitive polices enshrined within the tertiary institutions of the region discriminate against female students, with negative implications for female access to tertiary education.

The participation of female students in tertiary education is improving, albeit slowly, across SSA. In most SSA countries, the gender parity index—measured as the ratio of female to male enrollment—improved between 2000 and 2012. Relatively wealthy countries demonstrate fewer disparities than poorer countries of the region. In a subset of countries—Botswana, Cabo Verde, Lesotho, and Mauritius—female enrollment in higher education now outstrips male enrollment (figure 3.5). Although Lesotho continues to enjoy a gender parity index ratio of over 1, its index—as well as that of Angola, Mali, and Sudan—has worsened over the period.

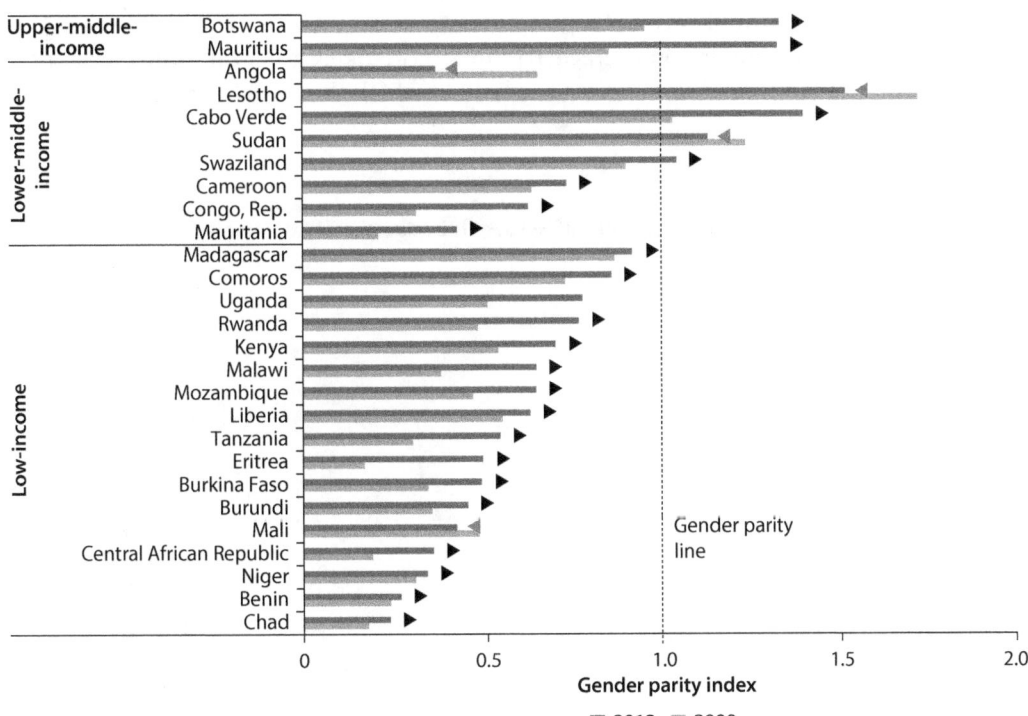

Figure 3.5 Tertiary GER Gender Parity Index in Selected Countries, 2000 and 2012

Source: World Bank EdSats.
Note: GER = gross enrollment ratio.

An additional concern regarding female participation in higher education is that, even in instances where female students are able to successfully access tertiary education, there is evidence of gender bias in the streaming of female students toward specific types of institutions and disciplines that are often associated with lower-paying jobs.

Parents' Education

Across virtually all countries for which data are available, the relationship between the socioeconomic status of parents and that of their adult offspring is positive and significant, across a range of measures of status (Hertz et al. 2007). Data from the latest round of SSA household surveys also demonstrate the persistence of the relationship between the education levels of parents and their children. The effects of poor intergenerational educational mobility reinforce social stratification, and the relative transmission of educational inequality from one generation to the next, serves as a proxy for a society's failure to provide opportunity to children from disadvantaged backgrounds.

Students from families where the head of household has had at least secondary education demonstrate significantly higher rates of participation in tertiary education than students from households in which the head of household did not complete primary education. Figure 3.6 illustrates how students from households where the head of household has at least completed secondary education are on average 10 times more likely to enroll in higher education than those born into a household in which the head of the household did

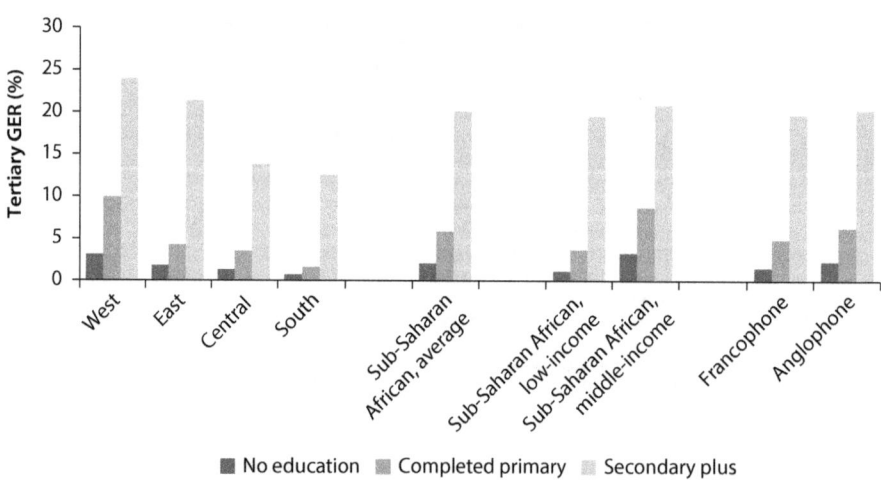

Figure 3.6 Tertiary GER by Head of Household's Educational Attainment

Source: Calculations are based on LSMS data.
Note: GER = gross enrollment ratio; SSA = Sub-Saharan Africa.

not complete primary education. Although subregional differences are evident in the data, this pattern of inequity is observable across all countries in SSA. Middle-income and Anglophone countries demonstrate relatively higher levels of equity; and, from a regional perspective, West Africa is marginally more equitable than other subregions.

Spatial and Regional Factors

There is a significant body of research that demonstrates that students from rural and deprived school districts are more likely to have limited access to quality pre-tertiary education. This further undermines their prospects for accessing tertiary education. The education status report for Malawi, for example, showed that, despite a large rural majority, the proportion of tertiary students from rural areas accounted for only 24 percent of total tertiary enrollment in 2007 (World Bank 2010). A similar study demonstrated that only 21 percent of students in the Rwandese tertiary education system came from rural areas in 2006 (World Bank 2011). Manuh, Gariba, and Budu (2007) conclude that in Ghana the most significant factor informing an individual's prospects for accessing university are the region and location of a student's residence. In Tanzania, two-thirds of tertiary enrollment is accounted for by 6 of the country's 22 administrative regions, and the 16 regions accounting for the remaining third of tertiary enrollment are disproportionately rural (Azcona et al. 2008). In Kenya, the pattern of the distribution of benefits associated with access to higher education is biased toward regions that have had a sitting president, with a concurrent bias in the distribution of public jobs (Mulongo 2013).

Urban and rural disparities perpetuate inequity in tertiary enrollment in a number of ways. Large urban centers are more likely to benefit from the presence of large and more established public tertiary institutions, which means that students from families residing in urban areas are more likely to have access to a larger variety of options for pursuing tertiary education. Urban areas are also more likely to benefit from pre-tertiary systems in which schools are better resourced and in which students demonstrate higher standardized test scores. These areas ultimately demonstrate higher tertiary enrollment rates. Compared with their rural counterparts, students in urban secondary schools are also more likely to benefit from access to information regarding tertiary admissions policies and from greater links between schools and university admission offices. Last, rural students face higher barriers to entry in the form of fees for housing because they are less likely to be able to commute from home to a university on a daily basis.

Students with Disabilities

There is very limited information available about disabled students' participation rates in tertiary education. Similarly, there is little research on the experience of disabled SSA students in higher education or on the presence of system wide interventions targeting the participation of disabled students for systems. One explanation for the apparent lack of emphasis on policies promoting the participation of disabled students in tertiary education is that there have been few opportunities for disabled people in low-income countries to effectively mobilize to assert their rights (Yeo 2005). There is some evidence that, in some SSA systems of tertiary education, access for disabled students to higher education in general, or in particular programs, is formally blocked or more informally discouraged (Howell 2005). Moreover, practices that exclude students with disabilities from basic education or segregate these students in nonacademic basic education limit the pool of students with disabilities who qualify for entry to institutions of higher education (Croft 2010).

In South Africa, 4,666 students with disabilities were enrolled in public institutions of higher education in 2009, equivalent to 0.6 percent of total tertiary enrollment and an increase from 4,325 students in 2007. This compares unfavorably with an estimated prevalence of disability of 3.5 percent within the South African cohort of those 20–29 years of age (Salmi and Bassett 2012).

The literature on the participation of students with disabilities in higher education suggests that their experience is colored by a range of barriers and frustrations specific to their relative disadvantage (Jacklin and Robinson 2007). Research conducted in Zimbabwe found that, although the University of Zimbabwe has facilitated the entry of students with disabilities since 1982, disabled students who were admitted experienced marginalization and disempowerment, including, but not limited to, negative stereotyping, difficulties with the admissions process, and inaccessible infrastructure (Chataika 2010). In Malawi, only 20 percent of educational institutions are wheelchair accessible (Loeb and Eide 2004).

The expansion of tertiary education systems in SSA has disproportionately benefited students drawn from the top income quintile of households, particularly in Francophone countries. Further patterns of inequity influencing access to tertiary education relate to gender, the level of educational achievement of the head of a student's household, location (rural versus urban), and disability.

In many instances, these patterns of inequity are interconnected and mutually reinforcing, with a direct impact on a student's prospect of accessing tertiary education. In order to address inequity in access to higher education, policies must incorporate a special emphasis on facilitating improved access of the most deprived social groups (for example, ethnic minority girls from the poorest families in rural areas), whose prospects for enrolling in tertiary education are particularly weak.

References

Azcona, G., R. D. Chute, L. Dookhony, H. Klein, D. Loyacano-Perl, D. Randazzo, and V. Reilly. 2008. *Harvesting the Future: The Case for Tertiary Education in Sub-Saharan Africa*. Syracuse: Maxwell School of Syracuse University.

Chataika, T. 2010. "Inclusion of Disabled Students in Higher Education in Zimbabwe." In *Cross-Cultural Perspectives on Policy and Practice: Decolonizing Community Contexts*, edited by J. Lavia and M. Moore. New York: Routledge.

Chimanikire, D. P. 2009. *Youth and Higher Education in Africa: The Cases of Cameroon, South Africa, Eritrea, and Zimbabwe*. Dakar: Council for the Development of Social Science Research in Africa.

Croft, A. 2010. *Including Disabled Children in Learning: Challenges in Developing Countries*. Project Report. Brighton, U.K.: Consortium for Research on Educational Access, Transitions and Equity.

Egbo, B. 2000. *Gender, Literacy, and Life Chances in Sub-Saharan Africa*. The Language and Education Library Series. Bristol, U.K.: Multilingual Matters.

Hertz, Tom, Tamara Jayasundera, Patrizio Piraino, Sibel Selcuk, Nicole Smith, and Alina Verashchagina. 2007. "The Inheritance of Educational Inequality: International Comparisons and Fifty-Year Trends." *B.E. Journal of Economic Analysis and Policy* 7 (2): 1–48.

Howell, C. 2005. *Higher Education Monitor: South Africa Higher Education Responses to Students with Disabilities—Equity of Access and Opportunity?* Pretoria: Council on Higher Education.

Jacklin, A., and C. Robinson. 2007. "What Is Meant by 'Support' in Higher Education? Towards a Model of Academic and Welfare Support." *Journal of Research in Special Educational Needs* 7 (2): 114–23.

Loeb, M., and A. Eide. 2004. *Living Conditions among People with Activity Limitations in Malawi: A National Representative Study*. Oslo: SINTEF Health Research.

Manuh, T., S. Gariba, and J. Budu. 2007. *Change and Transformation in Ghana's Publicly Funded Universities: A Study of Experiences, Lessons, and Opportunities*. Oxford: James Currey; Accra: Woeli Publishing Services.

Mulongo, G. 2013. "Inequality in Accessing Higher Education in Kenya; Implications for Economic Development and Well-Being." *International Journal of Humanities and Social Science* 3 (16).

Salmi, J., and R. M. Bassett. 2012. "Opportunities for All? The Equity Challenge in Tertiary Education." Salzburg Global Seminar Salzburg, Austria.

Yeo, R. 2005. *Disability, Poverty and the New Development Agenda*. Disability Knowledge and Research Programme. London: U.K. Department for International Development.

World Bank. 2010. *The Education System in Malawi*. Washington, DC: World Bank.

———. 2011. *Rwanda Education Country Status Report: Toward Quality Enhancement and Achievement of Universal Nine Year Basic Education*. Washington, DC: World Bank.

CHAPTER 4

Equity of Opportunities

Key Messages

- The majority of students in Sub-Saharan Africa (SSA) exit the education system at pre-tertiary levels. The poorer a student's household, the less likely that student is to enter pre-tertiary education at the appropriate and official age and to remain in school.
- Children from comparatively wealthy households disproportionately benefit from the rationing of free higher education because of their access to better-functioning schools, the increased likelihood that they will be exposed to academic role models, and other forms of cultural capital. Moreover, direct costs associated with tertiary education—such as tuition, housing, and food—and indirect costs relating to the opportunity cost of education impose a heavier burden on comparatively poor households.
- Lower-income families overestimate the opportunity costs associated with pursuing higher education (because of a higher share of forgone earnings, in terms of lower absolute incomes, in comparison to higher-income families).
- Lower-income families also underestimate the level of returns to job seekers with tertiary qualifications in the labor market.
- Differences in admission policies within SSA Francophone and Anglophone systems account for some of differences in equity outcomes.
- Information asymmetries exacerbate inequity in SSA tertiary systems because students from disadvantaged backgrounds are less likely than their wealthier peers to have access to accurate and up-to-date information regarding admissions processes, program selection, and the comparative labor market returns This negatively affects decision making with regard to program selection in higher education.

Inequity in Pre-Tertiary Levels of Education

The race for admission to universities commences at the kindergarten or pre-primary level. A significant body of research demonstrates higher levels of early childhood cognitive development for children born into wealthy families than for those born in less wealthy families. The less privileged a child's household circumstances, the less likely this child will be to commence his or her education at the official age for entry for schooling. Once students have entered the school system, their socioeconomic status strongly influences their prospects for continuing education, their likely level of educational attainment, and the extent to which their schooling will be delayed by grade repetition and extended absences from school. The United Nations Educational, Scientific, and Cultural Organization's Institute for Statistics (UIS) has demonstrated that children from the poorest quintile of households are four times more likely to be out of school than are children from the wealthiest quintile of households (40 percent versus 10 percent). These and other examples of inequity in pre-tertiary cycles of education significantly affect the composition of tertiary enrollment and the level of inequity in higher education.

Comparatively wealthy households are more likely to pay for private education in pre-tertiary education and to purchase the services of private tutors to prepare students for higher levels of education. A recent study of educational outcomes in Organisation for Economic Co-operation and Development (OECD) countries demonstrates that a student's academic performance is more strongly associated with the average socioeconomic status of other students' parents in the same school than by the socioeconomic status of a student's own parents (Causa and Johansson 2009).

Ghana, for example, has one of the best-performing basic educational systems in the region, yet only one-third of students demonstrate the level of proficiency in academic subjects (mathematics, sciences, language, and humanities) considered sufficient to access upper-secondary education. In Ghana, only (approximately) one-quarter of students start their upper-secondary education on time; and, of those who sit the examination to complete the upper-secondary cycle of education, more than half will fail the mathematics and sciences portions. Of those students who do successfully graduate from upper-secondary school, only one in five will continue on to tertiary education. As is typical in the majority of SSA countries, the successful transition to tertiary education is largely limited to a privileged few who attended the best secondary schools. This is underlined by evidence from Ghana, where approximately 70 percent of technical professionals with tertiary qualifications (for example, doctors, scientists, engineers, pharmacists) attended 18 of the country's 504 upper-secondary schools (Addae-Mensah 2000).

This book analyzes one manifestation of education inequity by measuring the mean years of schooling for individuals from the top income quintile as a ratio to the mean years for the rest of the population. The resulting ratio acts as a measure of the degree of inequity in a given education system. African students from households in the top quintile of income demonstrate 1.2 times more schooling than the remaining 80 percent of the households. Figure 4.1, below, illustrates that Francophone countries demonstrate a higher degree of inequity (with the ratio of mean years of schooling for individuals from the top income quintile over

Figure 4.1 Mean Years of Schooling for Population Ages 15–64 Years, Top 20 Percent versus Bottom 80 Percent, by Income

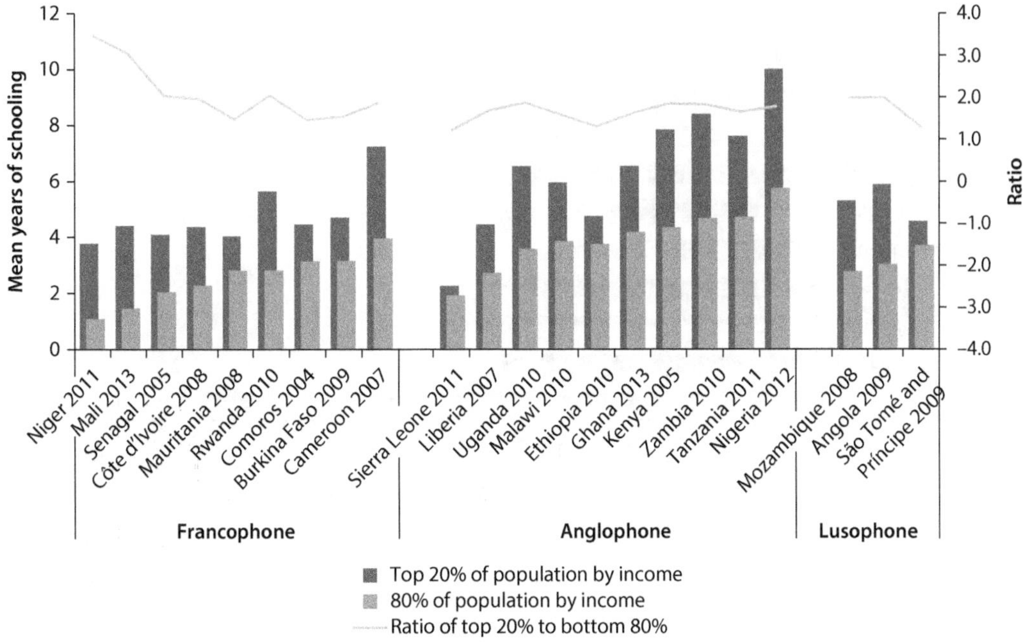

Source: Calculations are based on LSMS data.

mean years for the rest of the population ranging from 1.5 to 3.4), whereas Anglophone countries demonstrate lower levels disparity (with ratios ranging from 1.2 to 1.8). The distribution of mean years of schooling becomes even starker when the mean years of schooling for students from the top quintile of households is compared with that of students belonging to households from the bottom income quintile.

A comparison of this ratio over time demonstrates that Cameroon, Ghana, and Sierra Leone have significantly reduced inequity as measured in terms of mean educational attainment over the course of the past two decades (1990s to 2010s), with progress also evident in Ethiopia, Rwanda, and Uganda.[1] This measure of inequity has remained relatively constant in Côte d'Ivoire and Malawi but has worsened in Niger, Senegal, and Tanzania (figure 4.2).

Figure 4.3 illustrates tertiary enrollment per 100,000 inhabitants and inequity measured using the index constructed above. Countries located in the bottom right quadrant of the graph—such as Côte d'Ivoire, Malawi, Mozambique, and Niger—demonstrate high levels of inequity on the basis of comparative educational attainment and (low) enrollment. In these countries, inequity creates a bottleneck, requiring the system to expand if it is to catch up with the rest of the continent.

Figure 4.2 Inequity of Educational Attainment, 1990–2010

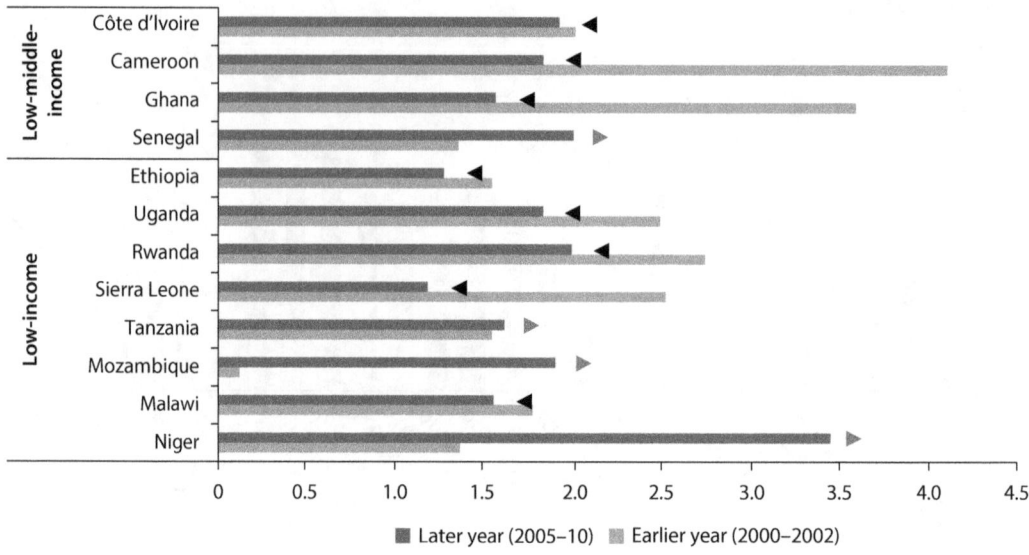

Source: Calculations are based on LSMS data.

Figure 4.3 Education Attainment Inequality Index and Tertiary Enrollment per 100,000 Inhabitants in Selected Sub-Saharan African Countries

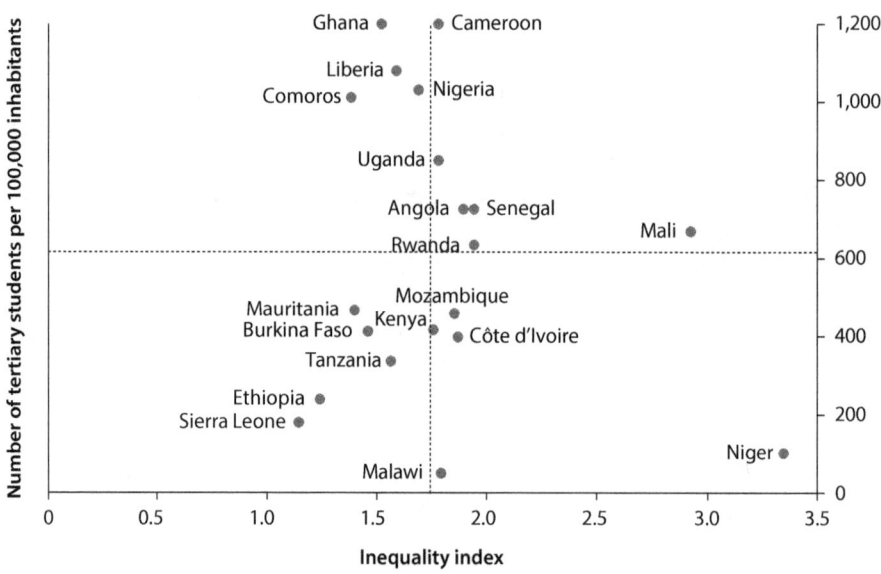

Source: Calculations are based on LSMS data.
Note: The inequality index measures educational attainment of the top 20 percent of the population versus the bottom 80 percent in terms of wealth. 0 = no inequality; 4 = high inequality.

Figure 4.4 and table 4.1 present data on the progression of students by income quintile through educational systems in Ghana and Rwanda. These two countries were chosen because Ghana is a West African Anglophone country, Rwanda is an East African Francophone country, and their educational systems are distinct in many ways.

Using Living Standard Measurement Study (LSMS) 2010 data, the mean years of schooling in Rwanda is approximately three years.[2] The data presented above demonstrate that attendance of students from households in the bottom 60 percent of income declines drastically toward the end of primary school. In grade 4, students from the poorest quintile of households account for 17 percent of attendance, but their numbers fall off rapidly to the extent that, by grade 7 (the first year of lower-secondary school), children from the poorest quintile of households account for only 7 percent of enrollment. By grade 10 (the first year of upper-secondary school), students from the poorest quintile of households account for just 2 percent of enrollment.

The government of Ghana has dedicated significant resources and policy attention to improving access to education, and this is evident in lower levels of disparity in pre-tertiary cycles of education. Using data from the 2013 Ghana Living Standards Survey (GLSS) Round 6, mean years of schooling in Ghana are approximately five years. The proportion of students from households in the bottom quintiles by income declines toward the end of lower-secondary school. Students from the poorest quintile of families outnumber their peers from the richest quintile throughout primary and lower-secondary school, with

Figure 4.4 Student Composition in Terms of Family Wealth Condition from Preschool to Tertiary-Level Education

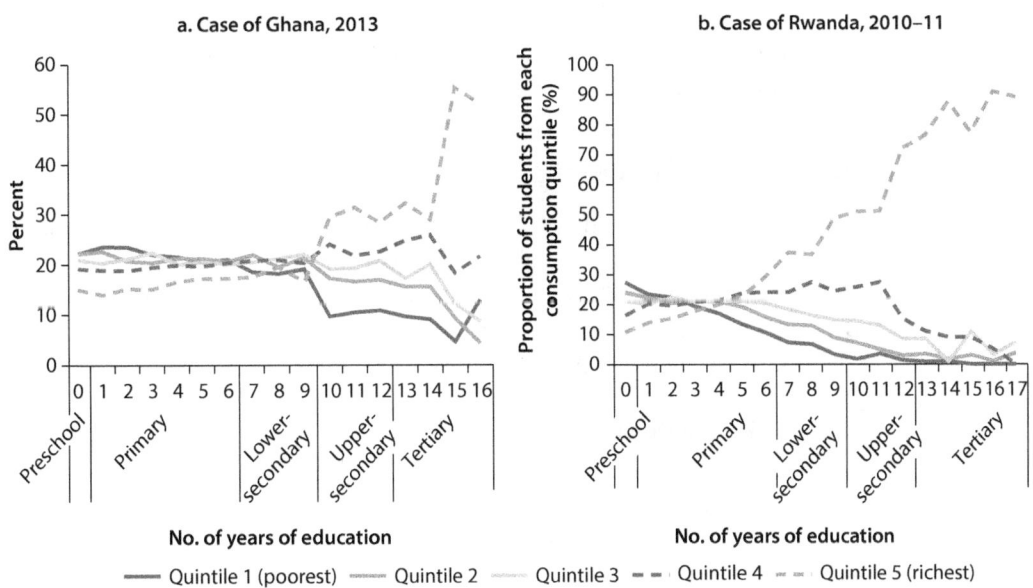

Table 4.1 Student Composition in Terms of Family Wealth Condition from Primary- to Tertiary-Level Education
percent

School Level	Grade	Quintile 1 (poorest)	Quintile 2	Quintile 3	Quintile 4	Quintile 5 (richest)
Case of Ghana, 2013						
Primary	4	22	21	20	20	17
	6	21	21	20	21	17
Lower-secondary	7	19	22	21	21	18
	9	19	21	22	20	17
Upper-secondary	10	10	17	19	24	30
	12	11	17	21	23	28
Tertiary	13	10	16	17	25	32
	17	13	4	9	22	52
Case of Rwanda, 2010–11						
Primary	4	17	21	21	21	20
	6	11	16	20	24	29
Lower-secondary	7	7	13	18	24	37
	9	3	9	15	24	49
Upper-secondary	10	2	7	14	26	51
	12	1	3	8	15	72
Tertiary	13	1	3	8	11	76
	17	0	4	7	0	89

Source: LSMS data.

the proportion of children from the highest quintile only surpassing that of the poorest quintile of households in grade 10 (the first year of upper-secondary school). From grade 10 and above, students from the richest quintile of households constitute a steadily increasing plurality of enrollment; however, at the tertiary level, students from the poorest quintile of households account for 10 percent of enrollment.

Costs of Pursuing Tertiary Education

The direct costs associated with tertiary education—for example, the costs of tuition, housing, and food—are obvious and tangible. Other costs, such as opportunity costs, are less obvious and are imposed indirectly. Taken together, direct and indirect costs constitute significant barriers to entry for comparatively poorer students in their choice to pursue tertiary education.

Out-of-Pocket Payments
Cost sharing refers to the practice of sharing the cost of tertiary education between governments (or taxpayers), parents, students, and philanthropists (Johnstone 2003). Internationally, there has been an increasing trend toward

greater cost sharing with regard to the costs of higher educational instruction and living costs. Historically, government funds have covered the majority of costs associated with higher education in SSA, and, in some cases, have provided tertiary education free of charge. Increasingly, these costs are being shared by governments, parents (or extended families), and students (Johnstone and Marcucci 2010). In 2009, at least 26 countries in Africa charged some form of upfront fees for tuition or other types of levies for tertiary education (for example, examination fees, registration fees, identity card fees, library fees, and information management system fees) (Experton and Fevere 2010).

In light of evidence demonstrating that tertiary graduates are more likely to accrue high earnings and benefit from increased social status, the practice of cost sharing is considered fair and efficient by its proponents. Johnstone (2003) captures the evidence and the ideological underpinnings of the support and opposition to the practice of cost sharing and concludes that this trend is likely inevitable and an outcome of the need for greater revenue by institutions and higher competition for public finance. Curtin (2000) contends that tertiary graduates who accrue higher earnings in the labor force are subject to higher income taxes, and these taxes offset the costs of the tertiary education from which they have benefited. However, governments in low-income countries tend to collect a relatively small share of revenue through personal income, wage, and consumption taxes (for example, a value-added tax) and, as a consequence, do not recover a significant proportion of costs expended on public education (Burgess 1997). Blaug (1992) asserts that any form of higher education subsidy involves a transfer of income from less-educated members of society to a more-educated stratum, from those who fail to accrue the full benefits of public education to those who do receive these benefits.

Countries that have introduced or raised user fees for access to tertiary education risk exacerbating inequity in the absence of effective and well-targeted financial aid mechanisms (Salmi et al. 2002). Tonheim and Matose (2013), for example, identify a lack of funding as the primary obstacle for young South Africans from disadvantaged socioeconomic backgrounds in accessing higher education.

In 2011, SSA households contributed an estimated 34 percent of national expenditures on higher education.[3] The share of household contributions as a share of total expenditures on tertiary education varies substantially, from a low of 13.6 percent in Chad to more than 50 percent in Benin, The Gambia, and Togo. Compared with high-income countries, households in low- and middle-income countries contribute the least to tertiary education—the most expensive level and the one where private returns to education are the highest (UNICEF 2015).

Research undertaken by the United Nations Educational, Scientific, and Cultural Organization (UNESCO) has demonstrated that the unit costs of education faced by households vary by level of education and progressively increase with each cycle of education from primary to higher education, equivalent to variation by a factor of 12. This trend is consistent across both public and private systems of education, although absolute unit costs are higher in private systems of education than in public systems. At the tertiary level, the wealthiest households' unit costs are over four times those of households from the two poorest quintiles (Foko, Tiyab, and Husson 2012).

Although the absolute value of investment in tertiary education is much larger for families from the richest quintiles of income, in many instances the cost of tertiary education, as measured by the share of education spending in household non-food-related expenditures, makes it unaffordable for poorer households (figure 4.5). In Ghana, for example, households in the bottom quintile of income must dedicate 37 percent of non-food-related expenditures to finance the cost of sending one child to a tertiary education institution. For these households, the share of non-food-related expenditures required to send one child to a university is twice that of households in the top quintile of income. This trend is also evident in the relative imposition of costs associated with secondary education on households. In Rwanda, the households in the poorest quintile of income must dedicate 51 percent of non-food-related expenditures for one child to pursue tertiary education, compared with 31 percent for households in the highest quintile of income. In this context, if a poor Rwandese family has more than one child who enrolls in tertiary education, mathematically the family has no capacity to invest in anything else.

Opportunity Costs and Forgone Earnings

In making the decision to pursue tertiary education, students must weigh the perceived costs of forgoing any current income against the perceived benefits of further education. Opportunity cost, in this context, is the stream of income that

Figure 4.5 Education Expenditures as a Percentage of Household Non–Food-Related Expenditures

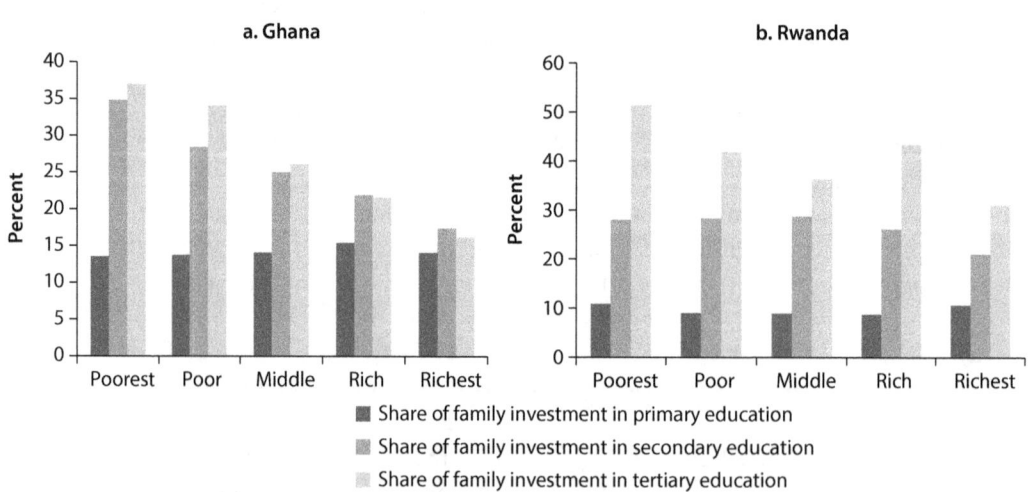

Source: Calculations are based on LSMS data.

students forgo by attending university as opposed to working. A good proxy of the value of this opportunity cost is the income of recent high school graduates in full-time employment. The opportunity cost of tertiary education typically weighs more heavily on poor households because the contribution of high-school graduates (in percentage terms, not absolute) to overall household income is higher than their peers from richer households (figure 4.6).

In general, increases in educational attainment are associated with increased income—with progressively higher jumps in earnings evident for upper-secondary and postsecondary graduates. In many countries, the earnings premium accruing to upper-secondary graduates is high, and they earn 100–150 percent more than people with no education. However, many labor markets in SSA lack mechanisms for appropriately appraising the market value of skill and merit. This erodes the market value of postsecondary qualifications. In Cameroon, Côte d'Ivoire, and Uganda, for example, workers with postsecondary qualifications do not earn significantly more than those who terminated their studies in the upper-secondary cycle. In Uganda, postsecondary graduates earn less than upper-secondary graduates. In Sierra Leone, workers with a primary education can earn more than workers who have completed secondary school. Despite a much larger earnings premium accruing to tertiary graduates in Sierra Leone, low returns to intermediate levels of education serve as a disincentive for students to continue their schooling.

Figure 4.6 Education and Private Income

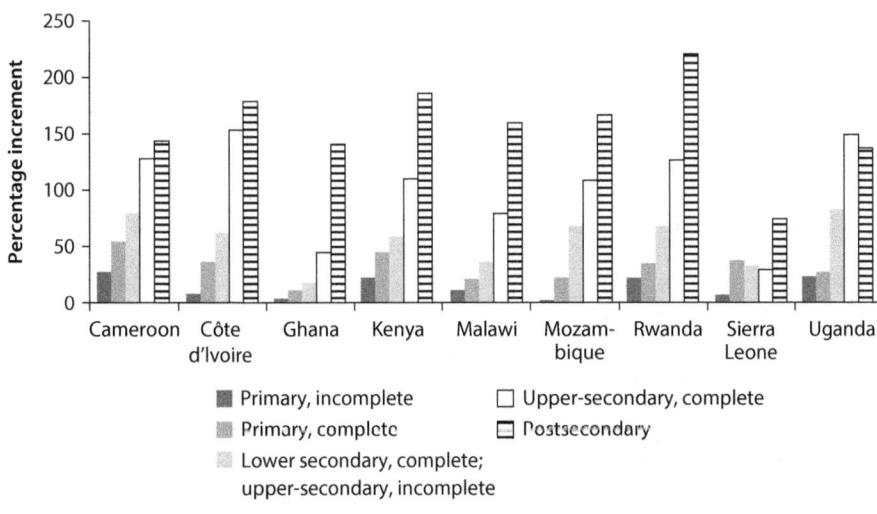

Source: Brooks et al. 2014.
Note: Simple average on standardized and harmonized household and labor force surveys. Based on a regression of hourly wages (in logs) by education level, adjusted for age, gender, and whether the workplace is urban or rural. Figure displays hourly wages among wageworkers by level of education (relative to workers without education). The dependent variable is ln (wage/hours) using information from the last seven days. Wages were adjusted for local consumer price index (2005 = 100) and purchasing power parity. This dependent variable was run against the dummy level of education variables listed above, and the "no education" dummy was excluded. As the mean wage among those with no education is normalized to zero, the wages shown are not absolute but are depicted in comparison to workers with no education. Workers ages 20–64 years.

Government Expenditures

Despite generally low levels of gross domestic product (GDP) per capita, African countries have generally managed to maintain consistent resource allocations in support of higher education (figure 4.7). Between 1998 and 2012, the countries of SSA allocated on average 0.8 percent of GDP, and approximately 18.5 percent of current public expenditures, to higher education.

Low- and lower-middle-income countries generally dedicate a relatively larger share of their total education budgets to primary education in support of efforts to achieve the Millennium Development Goal (MDG) of universal access to basic education. However, some countries allocate a disproportionally large share of total education expenditures to tertiary education. In Burkina Faso, the Central African Republic, Guinea, Mali, Senegal, and Tanzania, where the MDG of universal access to basic education is far from being achieved, more than 20 percent of total education expenditures are dedicated to tertiary education. The upper-middle-income countries of SSA generally allocate a much smaller proportion of total education spending to primary education.

A recent MDG report (UNECA et al. 2014) demonstrates that many countries on the African continent are on track to meet the MDG target for primary school enrollment, but much work remains to be done if these goals are to be reached. Twenty-five countries have now achieved net enrollment ratios of 80 percent or above, but primary completion rates remain relatively low. Twenty-eight percent of countries for which data are available demonstrate a completion rate below 60 percent. Moreover, approximately 22 percent of children of primary school age remain out of school, and a third of primary school students drop out without acquiring a basic proficiency in reading and mathematics. Despite significant progress toward the goal of achieving universal enrollment in primary education, much work remains to be done to ensure that all children in the region accrue the benefits of basic education.

Figure 4.7 Share of Government Spending, by Level of Education

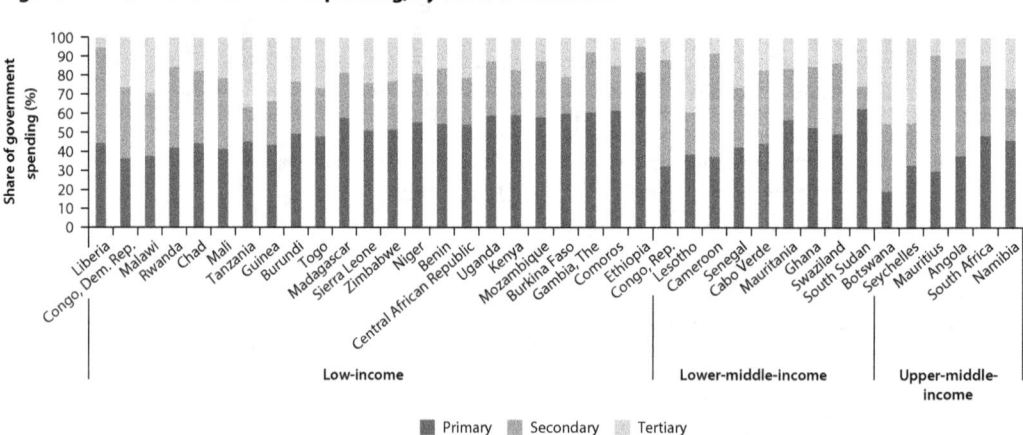

Source: World Bank EdStats.

Current levels of public expenditures on tertiary education in the region are insufficient to support the expansion in tertiary education required to meet increased demand. Given the magnitude of unmet needs at lower levels of education and in other social sectors, such as health and social protection, there is very little fiscal space for improving funding in support of the tertiary sector. The 2010 *Financing Higher Education in Africa* report concluded that, in a context wherein public funding is already overstretched, demand for tertiary education in SSA is growing significantly faster than the capacity to fund improved supply (Experton and Fevre 2010). Although current public expenditures dedicated to the higher education sector doubled between 1991 and 2006, increasing at an average annual rate of 6 percent each year, total enrollment in the sector tripled, from 2.7 million in 1991 in the same period, an average annual growth of 16 percent.

Financial constraints are further exacerbated by the high unit costs (per student expenditures) associated with delivering higher education. From a regional perspective, the ratio of the unit cost of tertiary education to the unit cost of primary education—that is, the relative expensiveness of tertiary education compared with primary education—for SSA is highest in the world (figure 4.8). In general, the average cost of educating one university graduate is equivalent to the cost of educating 14.5 primary school students in SSA, compared with 2.2 for the rest of the world. Spending in support of each student enrolled in tertiary education in Chad, Kenya, Swaziland, and Zambia, for example, is equivalent to 150 percent of GDP per capita; and in no SSA country does spending on a primary school student exceed 24 percent of GDP

Figure 4.8 Public Expenditures per Tertiary Student over the Costs of Educating One Student in Primary School, SSA and Countries with Similar Profile

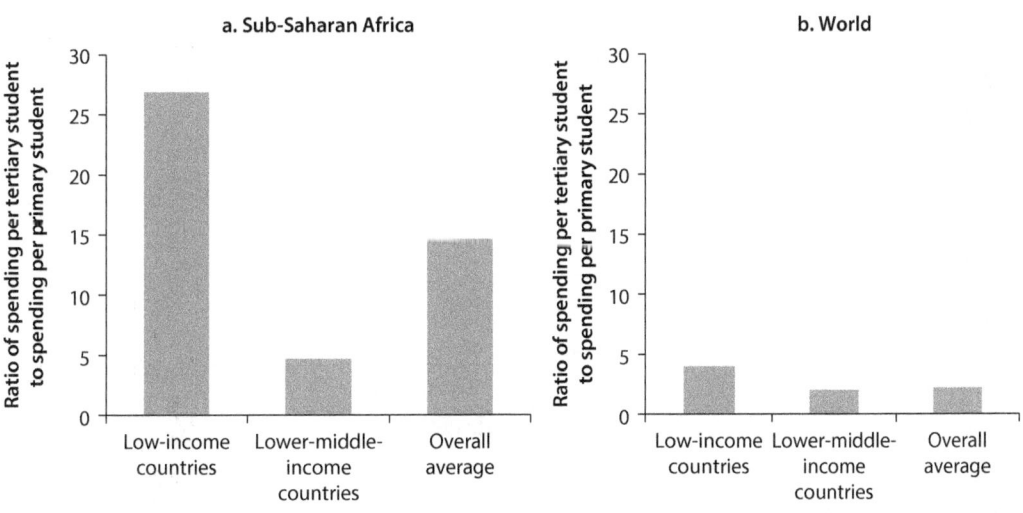

Source: UIS data.

per capita. In low-income SSA counties the average unit cost for tertiary education is 26.6 times that for primary education. In an extreme case such as Malawi, public spending per tertiary student is 225 times that for a single student enrolled in primary school.

SSA is the only region in the world that has seen a decrease in public expenditures per student in support of tertiary education. However, those decreasing expenditures do not result from increased efficiency in the systems of the continent but rather from increasing university austerity. Practices such as linking enrollment to the number of beds available in university hostels have been pursued in some countries. Austerity has resulted in overcrowded classrooms, rising student–teacher ratios, limits on student access to computers and laboratory facilities, the deterioration of infrastructure, and lower levels of support for academic research. A recent World Bank study demonstrated the extent to which infrastructure is under strain in the region: in an analysis of public tertiary facilities based on an intended theoretical enrollment of 100 students, average actual enrollment in Benin was 350 in 2007, in Cameroon it was 220 in 2006, and in the Central African Republic it was 260 in 2007 (Experton and Fevre 2010).

Figure 4.9 illustrates that countries with relatively better-developed tertiary education systems have lower current public expenditures per student enrolled in tertiary education compared with current public expenditures per primary student. The high unit costs associated with tertiary education in SSA have constrained the expansion of systems and have limited efforts to catch up with other regions.

Figure 4.9 Ratio of Current Public Expenditures per Tertiary Student to Current Public Expenditures per Primary Student, SSA versus Non-SSA Countries

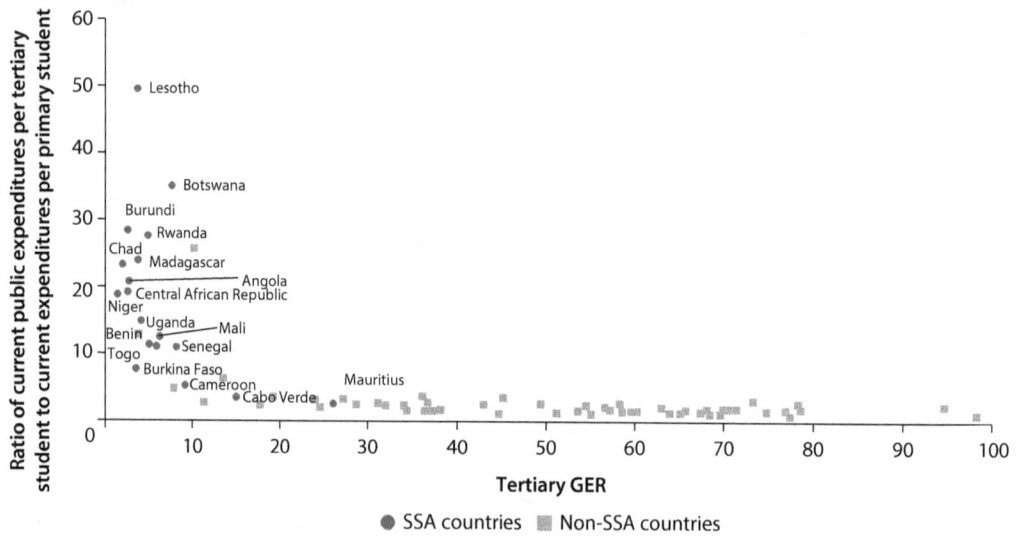

Source: UNESCO 2011.
Note: GER = gross enrollment ratio; SSA = Sub-Saharan Africa; UNESCO = United Nations Educational, Scientific, and Cultural Organization.

Inefficient management practices and systems divert scarce resources from funding interventions to achieve the objectives of improving access, delivering quality education, and increasing the relevance of tertiary education (Salmi et al. 2002). Recurrent expenditures accounted for more than 90 percent of total spending in support of tertiary education in 18 of 27 countries for which data were available in 2012 (figure 4.10). Public expenditures on salaries range from 17.5 percent in Rwanda to over 90 percent in the Democratic Republic of the Congo (figure 4.11). The higher the proportion of total spending apportioned to salaries, the lower the share of resources available to support other interventions, such as funding financial aid for students from disadvantaged backgrounds. In many systems, once a new hire is approved, payment of the associated salary is the responsibility of government. In these systems, there is no incentive for institutions to initiate administrative reforms or to make their payroll more efficient.

Historically, many SSA governments have supported the costs of students in pursuing tertiary education abroad, resulting in problems of equity and loss

Figure 4.10 Recurrent Expenditures as a Percentage of Total Expenditures in Tertiary Public Institutions

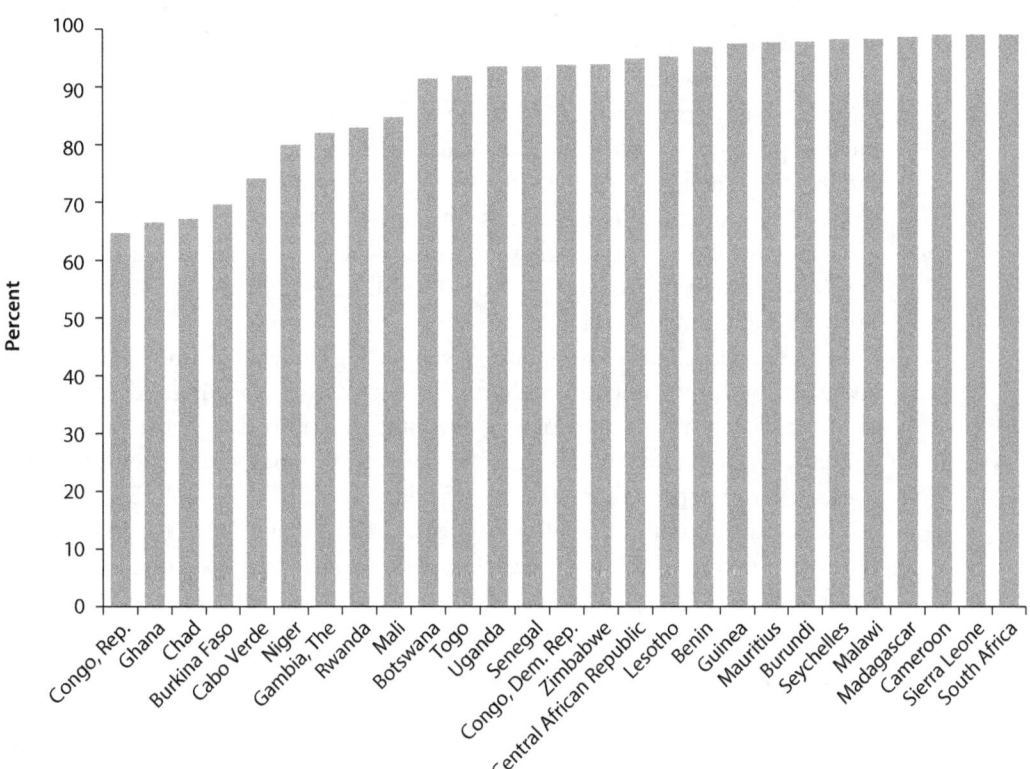

Source: UIS data.
Note: UIS = United Nations Educational, Scientific, and Cultural Organization Institute for Statistics.

Figure 4.11 Total Salaries as a Share of Total Expenditures in Tertiary Public Institutions, Selected SSA Countries

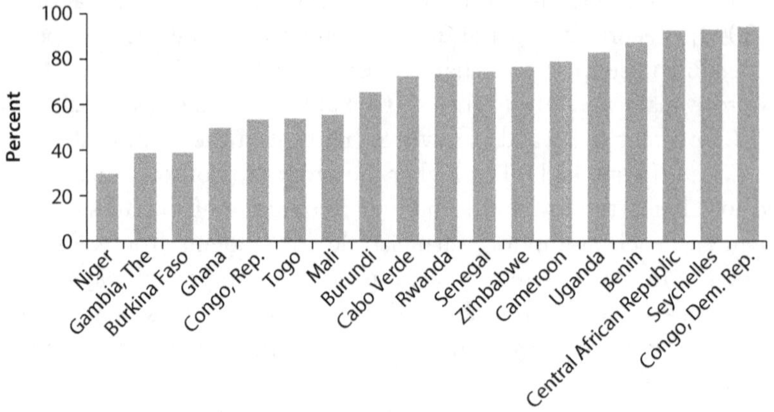

Source: UIS data.
Note: Data are from 2012 or the latest year available. SSA = Sub-Saharan Africa; UIS = United Nations Educational, Scientific, and Cultural Organization Institute for Statistics.

of talent. These programs divert scarce resources away from the expansion of local systems of tertiary education and have traditionally benefited only a small group of high-performing or well-connected students. A significant number of individuals who are supported in pursuing tertiary study abroad never return, depriving their countries of the skills and knowledge development supported by public monies. Many view the subsequent "brain drain" as the biggest challenge to development. The brain drain phenomenon also comes at considerable financial cost; it has been estimated, for example, that SSA spends US$4 billion each year to support the salaries of approximately 100,000 Western expatriates who help to fill the gap in the supply of professionals (Teichler and Yagci 2009).

In recent years, public expenditures supporting students to study abroad have decreased, and governments should further decrease scholarship funds in support of external study. The ratio of students studying abroad to those enrolled in domestic tertiary institutions, also known as the outbound mobility ratio, decreased from 6 percent in 2003 to 4.5 percent in 2012 (figure 4.12). However, SSA's current outbound mobility ratio is still more than double the global average of 1.8 percent, and more than four times the outbound mobility ratio for South and West Asia.

Benefit Incidence Analysis

The argument informing the public subsidization of tertiary education is that, in imperfect markets such as those prevalent in many SSA countries, people are more inclined to underinvest in tertiary education if they do not have the capacity to correctly assess its costs and benefits. Moreover, without

Figure 4.12 Outbound Mobility Ratio, 2013

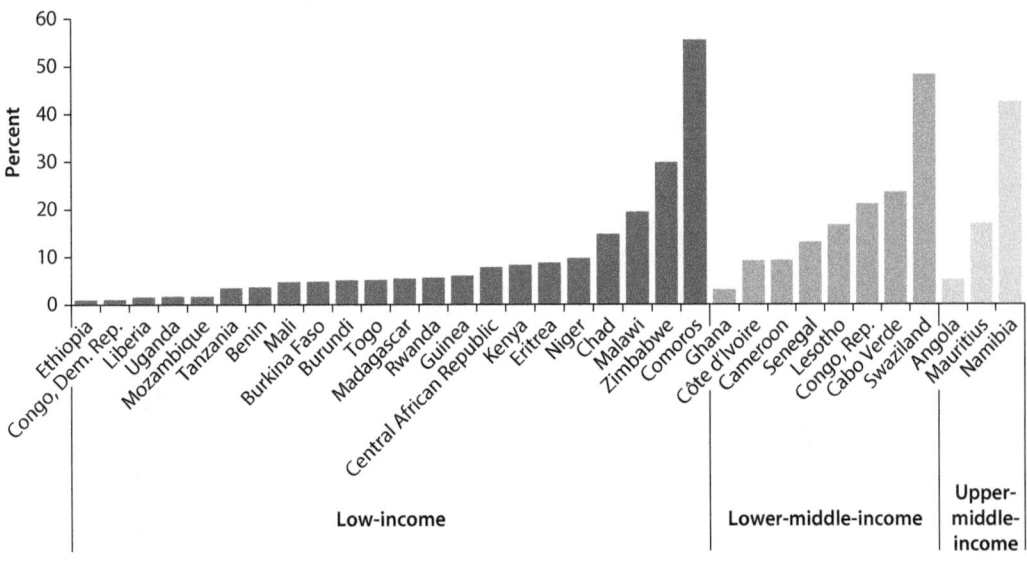

Source: UIS data.
Note: UIS = United Nations Educational, Scientific, and Cultural Organization Institute for Statistics.

a government subsidy, the families of qualified but poor students may not be able to borrow to finance school attendance. In systems where tertiary education is funded predominantly through government funds and a substantial private tertiary sector is absent, inequity is perpetuated when (i) participation in higher educational is low; (ii) the children of the wealthy and powerful disproportionately benefit from the rationing of free higher education as a consequence of their access to better schools in pre-tertiary cycles of education, increased access to academic role models, and other forms of cultural capital; and (iii) the distribution of taxes used to support "free" higher education is proportional or even regressive across taxpayers in terms of relative wealth (Johnstone 2004).

Inequity in the distribution of public expenditures in support of tertiary education can be illustrated using the Lorenz curve. The Lorenz curve shows the distribution of resources allocated within a given population by income. If resources are distributed equally across all members of a population, the resulting Lorenz curve would be a straight line with a slope of 45 degrees. The Lorenz curves illustrated in figure 4.13 demonstrate the inequitable distribution of public expenditures on tertiary education in Ghana, Malawi, Mali, Rwanda, Tanzania, and Uganda. In Rwanda, more than 80 percent of government spending on tertiary education accrues to 20 percent of the population.

A Gini coefficient for education can be derived from the Lorenz curve, with the area between perfect equality (the 45-degree line) and the Lorenz curve constituting the numerator, and the area below the 45-degree line serving as

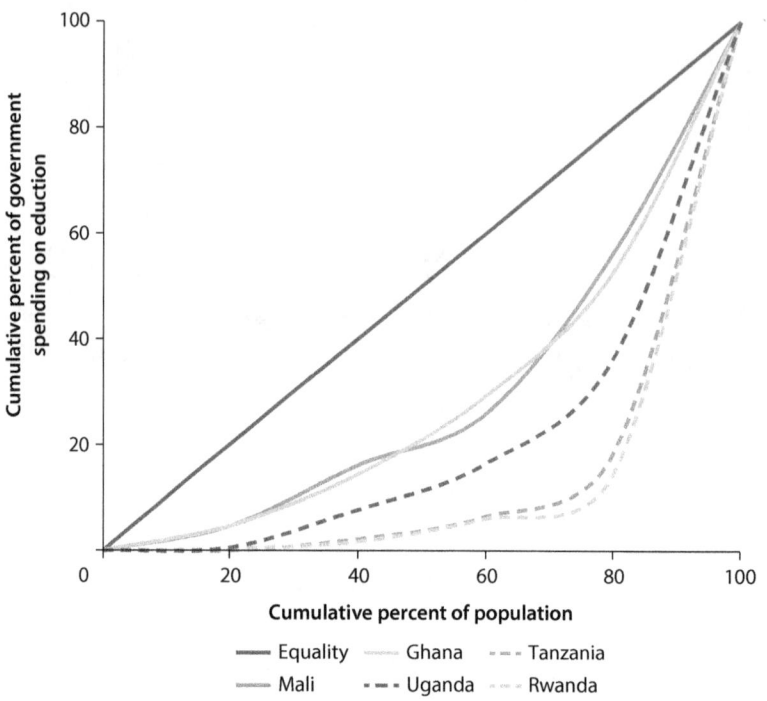

Figure 4.13 Lorenz Curves for Incidence of Public Expenditures in Tertiary Education in Ghana, Mali, Rwanda, Tanzania, and Uganda

Source: LSMS data.
Note: Data are from 2011 or the most recent year available.

Table 4.2 Education Gini Coefficients in Ghana, Mali, Tanzania, and Malawi

Education level	Ghana (2013)	Mali (2013)	Tanzania (2011)	Malawi (2011)
Tertiary	0.41	0.40	0.69	0.74
Upper-secondary	0.23	0.35	0.38	0.52
Lower-secondary	0.08	0.12	—	0.32
Primary	0	0	0.13	0

Source: LSMS data.
Note: — = not available.

the denominator. An education Gini coefficient ranges from 0 to 1, with 0 indicating perfect equality and 1 perfect inequality. An analysis of education Gini coefficients across levels of education from primary to tertiary demonstrates the significant impact of improved pro-poor expenditures on support for basic education. The Gini coefficients for primary education collated in table 4.2 are close to 0; however, inequity increases with each level of education, and the highest levels of inequality are evident for tertiary education.

Tertiary Admissions Policies

The legacy of colonialism is evident in the different admissions systems used in Francophone and Anglophone countries. For a range of reasons, French colonial schools were generally more elitist (Gifford and Weiskel 1971). Teaching in Francophone countries was performed in French, whereas the British more commonly used vernacular languages for teaching in their educational systems. French colonies provided free education, which resulted in a concentration of expenditures in a limited number of schools. Education in French colonies was, by law, secular, whereas British administrations encouraged and subsidized missionary schools. These and other factors resulted in relatively decentralized systems of education in Anglophone countries, allowing for greater leeway with regard to local languages and religion. On the other hand, the French colonial school system was designed to educate a small elite, disproportionately concentrated in the colonial capital or other urban centers, as opposed to institutionalizing mass education. The French colonial system also imposed stricter controls on curricula, school management, and instructional language use, with the state assuming an almost exclusive (and expensive) role as a provider of education (Cogneau and Moradi 2014).

Contemporary Francophone systems are highly selective in pre-tertiary cycles of education; however, once a student obtains a *baccalauréat*, the qualification earned by a high school graduate, he or she has the right to enter higher education supported by generous government subsidies. With the exception of a few colleges that limit student admissions and institutions with a competitive admissions process, such as the University of Niamey in Niger and the University of Antananarivo in Madagascar, higher education institutions in Francophone systems generally do not implement selective admissions processes (Gioan 2008).

In contrast, Anglophone countries generally have selective admissions policies for tertiary education. In Liberia, for example, admission is based solely on a student's performance on the West African Examinations Council (WAEC) 12th grade examinations and university entrance examinations.

However, merit-based admissions policies do not usually take a student's socioeconomic background into account, on the assumption that talented students from disadvantaged backgrounds will find their way into the system on the basis of merit. In practice, students from urban and wealthy families are disproportionate beneficiaries of these admissions policies. Atuahene and Ansah (2013) demonstrate, for example, that in Ghana students who attended one of the country's top-ranked secondary schools (staffed with quality teachers and comparatively better equipped) tend to perform better than their peers who attended schools in rural and historically disadvantaged regions of the country (schools more likely to be characterized by suboptimal academic inputs and facilities).

Countries such as Ghana, Kenya, and Uganda have implemented a dual fee-paying and subsidized admission policy. In these contexts, an applicant who meets the basic qualifications for entry to tertiary education but has not been admitted to an academic program because of the competitive "cut-off" for admission can enroll in a public university on a fee-paying basis. Given the strong correlation between academic performance in pre-tertiary cycles of education and family wealth, it is unlikely that most students from less-advantaged backgrounds benefit from this approach.

Another factor that disproportionately affects students from poorer households is the lack of easily accessible information regarding admissions processes, program selection, and the comparative labor market returns to programs of tertiary study. Ajayi (2013) demonstrates that in Ghana, when primary school students are able to apply to a limited number of secondary schools prior to knowing their test scores, students in lower-performing elementary schools are more likely to limit their secondary school preference to schools in close proximity to their home. They are also less likely to have a high-performing secondary school located in their home district. An analysis of the Kenyan tertiary admissions system demonstrates that, with limited information on the quality of junior high schools and their admissions processes, children and parents make judgment errors in the selection process; and these informational constraints are more acute for students from more-disadvantaged backgrounds (Glennerster et al. 2011). A comparative case study analysis of seven East African universities demonstrated a disconnect between secondary schools and public universities in the sharing of admissions and program information and in preparing new students, with students in rural secondary schools more likely to be relatively uninformed (Griffin 2007). Poor information regarding the link between program choice and the labor market returns accruing to programs of study increases the risk of dropouts at the tertiary level.

Notes

1. Calculated as the ratio in mean years of schooling between the richest 20 percent of the population and mean years of schooling of the remaining 80 percent of the population.
2. Preschool is counted as 0 years of schooling.
3. Simple average.

References

Addae-Mensah, I. 2000. *Education in Ghana: A Tool for Social Mobility or Social Stratification?* J. B. Danquah Memorial Lectures. Accra: Ghana Academy of Arts and Sciences.

Ajayi, K. F. 2013. "School Choice and Educational Mobility: Lessons from Secondary School Applications in Ghana." IED Working Paper. http://people.bu.edu/kajayi/Ajayi_EducationalMobility.pdf.

Atuahene, F., and A. Owusu-Ansah. 2013. "A Descriptive Assessment of Higher Education Access, Participation, Equity, and Disparity in Ghana." *SAGE Open*. July–August. 1–16. http://journals.sagepub.com/doi/pdf/10.1177/2158244013497725.

Blaug, M. 1992. "The Overexpansion of Higher Education in the Third World." In *Equity and Efficiency in Economic Development: Essays in Honour of Benjamin Higgins*, edited by D. J. Savoie and I. Brecher, 232–44. Montreal: McGill–Queen's University Press.

Brooks, K. M., D. P. Filmer, M. L. Fox, A. Goyal, T. A. Mengistae, P. Premand, D. Ringold, S. Sharma, and S. Zorya. 2014. *Youth Employment in Sub-Saharan Africa*. Washington, DC: World Bank.

Burgess, R. S. 1997. "Fiscal Reform and the Extension of Basic Health and Education Coverage." In *Marketizing Education and Health in Developing Countries*, edited by C. Colclough. New York: Clarendon Press, Oxford University Press.

Causa, O., and A. Johansson. 2009. *Intergenerational Social Mobility*. Paris: OECD Publishing.

Cogneau, D., and A. Moradi. 2014. "Borders That Divide: Education and Religion in Ghana and Togo since Colonial Times." *Journal of Economic History* 74 (3): 694–729.

Curtin, T. 2000. "All Taxes Are Graduate Taxes: How the Tax System Delivers Automatic Recovery of Government Spending on Higher Education." *The Round Table* 89 (356): 479–91.

Experton, William, and Chloe Fevre. 2010. *Financing Higher Education in Africa*. Directions in Development Series. Washington, DC: World Bank.

Foko, B., B. K. Tiyab, and G. Husson. 2012. *Household Education Spending: An Analytical and Comparative Perspective for 15 African Countries*. Dakar: UNESCO/Dakar and Pôle de Dakar.

Gifford, P., and T. C. Weiskel. 1971. "African Education in a Colonial Context: French and British Styles." In *France and Britain in Africa, Imperial Rivalry and Colonial Rule* edited by P. Gifford, and W. R. Louis, 663–711. New Haven, CT: Yale University Press.

Gioan, A. P. 2008. *Higher Education in Francophone Africa: What Tools Can Be Used to Support Financially-Sustainable Policies?* Washington, DC: World Bank.

Glennerster, R. E, M. Kremer, I. Mbiti, and K. Takavarasha. 2011. *Access and Quality in the Kenyan Education System: A Review of the Progress, Challenges and Potential Solutions*. Nairobi: Office of the Prime Minister of Kenya.

Griffin, A.-M. 2007. *Educational Pathways in East Africa: Scaling a Difficult Terrain*. Kampala: Association for the Advancement of Higher Education and Development (AHEAD).

Johnstone, D. B. 2003. "Cost-Sharing in Higher Education: Tuition, Financial Assistance, and Accessibility in a Comparative Perspective." *Czech Sociological Review* 39 (3): 351–74.

———. 2004. "Cost-Sharing and Equity in Higher Education: Implications of Income Contingent Loans." *Higher Education Dynamics* 6: 37–59.

Johnstone, D. B., and P. Marcucci. 2010. *Financially Sustainable Student Loan Programs: The Management of Risk in the Quest for Private Capital*.

Salmi, J., B. Millot, D. Court, M. Crawford, P. Darvas, F. Golladay, L. Holm-Nielsen, R. Hopper, A. Markov, P. Moock, H. Mukherjee, W. Saint, S. Shrivastava, F. Steier, and R. van Meel. 2002. *Constructing Knowledge Societies*. Directions in Development Series. Washington, DC: World Bank.

Teichler, U., and Y. Yagci, Y. 2009. "Changing Challenges of Academic Work: Concepts and Observations." In *Higher Education, Research and Innovation: Changing Dynamics*, edited by V. L. Meek, U. Teichler, and M. Kearney, 85–145. Kassel, Germany: International Centre for Higher Education Research.

Tonheim, Milfrid, and Frank Matose. 2013. "South Africa: Social Mobility for a Few?" NOREF Report, Norwegian Peacebuilding Resource Centre, Oslo, October.

UIS (United Nations Educational, Scientific and Cultural Organization Institute for Statistics). 2012. "Reaching Out-of-School Children Is Crucial for Development." *Education for All Global Monitoring Report*, Policy Paper 04, UNESCO, Paris.

UNECA (United Nations Economic Commission for Africa), African Union, African Development Bank, and United Nations Development Programme. 2014. *MDG Report 2014: Assessing Progress in Africa toward the Millennium Development Goals*. Addis Ababa: UNECA, African Union, African Development Bank, and United Nations Development Programme.

UNESCO (United Nations Educational, Scientific, and Cultural Organization). 2011. *Financing Education in Sub-Saharan Africa: Meeting the Challenges of Expansion, Equity and Quality*. Montreal: UNESCO Institute for Statistics.

UNICEF (United Nations Children's Fund). 2015. *The Investment Case for Education and Equity*. New York: UNICEF.

CHAPTER 5

Equity of Outcomes

Key Messages
- Tertiary education yields substantial market and nonmarket benefits for both the individual and society.
- Tertiary education accrues the highest private returns of any level of education.
- Research demonstrates that the returns to education for female workers are generally higher than for male workers.
- In general, public returns to education are smaller than private returns because of the inclusion of public costs. Social returns are difficult to measure and attribute.
- There is significant country-level variance in the magnitude of tertiary education benefits accruing to students from comparatively poor households. However, students from comparatively poor households are also likely to benefit the most from tertiary education.

The previous chapters demonstrated how (i) various forms of exclusion contribute to low transition rates in pre-tertiary cycles of education, with many students unable to accrue the credentials required for admission to tertiary education; (ii) the high costs associated with education—including fees, living costs, and opportunity costs—can be prohibitive in the context of accessing tertiary education; (iii) the suboptimal targeting of public subsidies for tertiary education disproportionately benefits relatively wealthy students; and (iv) information asymmetries regarding the benefits (and costs) of tertiary education prevent many students from optimizing educational investment choices. This chapter discusses what happens when tertiary students graduate, and it attempts to explain disparities in outcomes through the following frames of analysis: (i) the private, public, and social returns to tertiary education; and (ii) the impact of tertiary education on social mobility.

Private Returns to Tertiary Education

Access to tertiary education generates strong private returns. The analysis in this chapter suggests that tertiary graduates generally experience improved opportunities for employment and have higher incomes. The most common method for measuring the benefits accruing to individuals with different levels of education is a Mincerian estimate of private rates of return to education. The estimate compares increases in an individual's income, associated with the completion of an additional year of schooling or a higher level of education, and the increased costs associated with further education. In general, workers with higher levels of education have higher incomes. This formula takes into account the full private costs (forgone earnings or opportunity costs, and direct costs such as tuition or fees) and private benefits (posttax earnings).

Over the past four decades, an increasing body of knowledge has been amassed on the empirical study of patterns of estimated returns to education in developing economies (table 5.1). A recent World Bank report by Montenegro and Patrinos (2014) concludes that, in the economies of Sub-Saharan Africa (SSA):

- Returns to education are very high for tertiary and primary education, with significant, but smaller, returns to education evident at the secondary level.
- Returns to education are higher in low-income economies than in higher-income economies.
- Estimated returns to education are higher for women than for men, especially in SSA.
- Despite rising levels of average educational attainment, the returns to education have declined modestly over time, suggesting that the net demand for skills has increased with the net supply of skills.

Table 5.1 Average Returns to Schooling, by Education Level and Gender

Region	Total			Male			Female			No. of countries
	Primary	Secondary	Tertiary	Primary	Secondary	Tertiary	Primary	Secondary	Tertiary	
East Asia	13.6	5.3	14.8	12.6	5.8	15.0	9.5	6.4	15.8	13
Europe and Central Asia	13.9	4.7	10.3	12.1	4.2	9.8	11.9	6.4	12.2	20
Latin America	7.8	5.4	15.9	7.9	5.3	15.7	8.7	6.5	17.4	23
Middle East and NorthAfrica	16.0	4.5	10.5	12.7	4.3	10.2	21.4	7.4	13.5	10
South Asia	6.0	5.0	17.3	4.7	3.9	16.6	4.8	6.2	23.3	7
Sub-Saharan Africa	14.4	10.6	21.0	12.5	10.1	21.0	17.5	12.7	21.3	33
Low-income countries	13.4	9.2	10.7	8.1	16.3	15.7	14.7	11.7	15.7	34
All economies	11.5	6.8	14.6	10.1	6.7	14.4	13.2	8.2	16.1	139

Source: Montenegro and Patrinos 2014.
Note: Data are from the most recent reporting period for each country.

There is a significant consensus among scholars that private returns accruing to tertiary graduates in SSA are larger than those observed in other regions (see box 5.1). Montenegro and Patrinos (2014) demonstrate that, over the past two decades, earnings for tertiary graduates in countries such as Burkina Faso, Ghana, Madagascar, Malawi, and South Africa have consistently increased. This outcome is associated with a context in which the supply of tertiary degree holders remains insufficient to meet increasing labor market demand for relevant skills. On the other hand, private returns to primary education have gradually decreased in SSA as the supply of workers with primary education has increased, despite a concurrent increase in the private returns associated with secondary and tertiary education.

Box 5.1 Does Higher Educational Attainment Lead to Higher Private Returns? The Case of the Democratic Republic of Congo

After decades of conflict and war, a critical component of the Democratic Republic of Congo's efforts to secure a lasting peace and improve economic growth entails interventions to improve the productivity of its workforce. This requires an understanding on the part of policy makers regarding the relationship between the country's supply of and demand for skills and the adoption of policies to maximize the benefits of human capital.

Table B5.1.1 below tabulates the mean years of educational attainment for subgroups of the population between 15 and 64 years of age (a proxy for the country's labor force). Mean educational attainment for the entire labor force is 6.6, with male workers demonstrating, on average, almost three more years of education than female workers. Moreover, urban workers demonstrate 4.2 more years of schooling than their rural peers.

As demonstrated by table B5.1.2, the annual opportunity costs associated with upper-secondary and tertiary education are significantly higher than those associated with primary and lower secondary. According to the World Development Indicators database, adjusted net national income per capita (current US$) in the Democratic Republic of Congo in 2012 was approximately US$220.[a] This is below the estimated opportunity cost for upper-secondary education and is one-third of the estimated opportunity cost associated with tertiary education. As a consequence, accessing advanced cycles of education remains extremely costly, if not prohibitively expensive, for the majority of citizens.

Table B5.1.1 Average Schooling Statistics in the Democratic Republic of Congo

Statistic	Average no. of years of schooling
Total population	6.6
Male	8.0
Female	5.3
Urban areas	9.1
Rural areas	4.9

Source: Darvas et al. 2016.
Note: Data are for those ages 15–64 years, representing the country's working-age population.

box continues next page

Box 5.1 Does Higher Educational Attainment Lead to Higher Private Returns? The Case of the Democratic Republic of Congo *(continued)*

On the basis of an analysis of household survey data, tertiary education accrues the highest private returns, at approximately 20 percent. Research demonstrates that the returns to education for female workers are generally higher than for male workers. However, in the case of the Democratic Republic of Congo, this is true only for levels of education above lower secondary. Figure B5.1.1 illustrates average private returns associated with an additional year of schooling and with each level of education. The data also demonstrate that returns to education are much higher for workers in urban areas than for workers in rural areas, and this holds true when considering an additional year of schooling and at each level of education.

The premium accruing to education varies significantly by region, as illustrated in figure B5.1.2. For example, the Katanga region demonstrates the highest return for an additional year of schooling. Returns to education also differ with regard to which level of education demonstrates

Table B5.1.2 Estimated Opportunity Cost, by Level of Education

Education level	Estimated annual opportunity cost (in CGF)
Primary	44,319
Lower-secondary	77,046
Upper-secondary	256,202
Tertiary	673,204

Source: Darvas et al. 2016.
Note: CGF = Congo franc.

Figure B5.1.1 Summary of Returns to Education

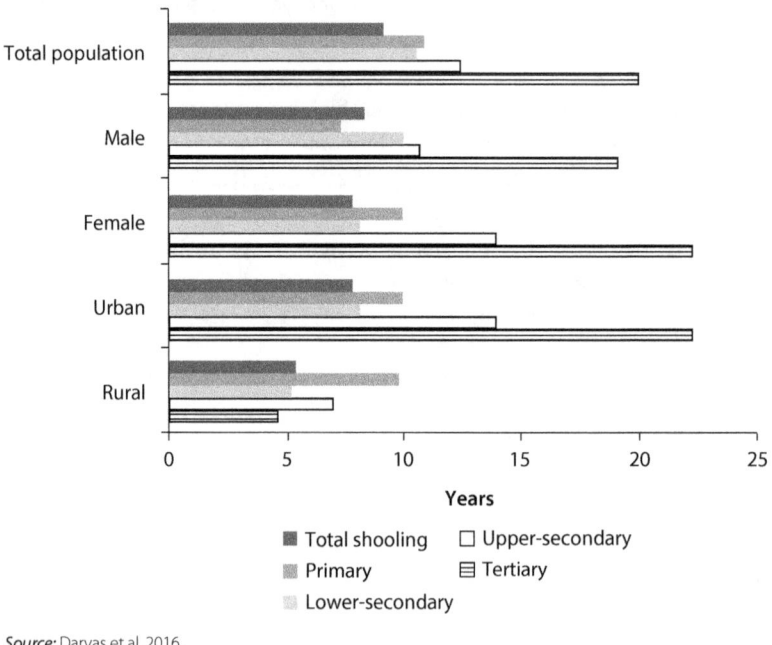

Source: Darvas et al. 2016.

box continues next page

Box 5.1 Does Higher Educational Attainment Lead to Higher Private Returns? The Case of the Democratic Republic of Congo *(continued)*

Figure B5.1.2 Returns to Education, by Province

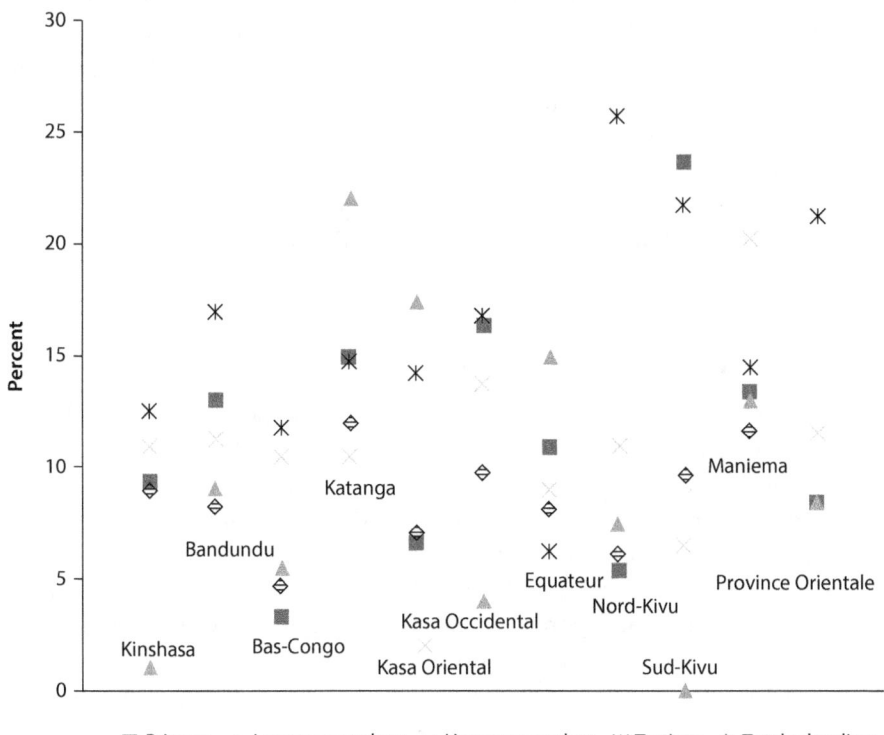

Source: Darvas et al. 2016.

the highest premium. In 6 of the country's 11 provinces, the highest returns are associated with tertiary education; however, secondary education is the most profitable investment in Katanga, Kasa Oriental, Equateur, and Maniema, and primary education shows the highest returns in Sud-Kivu. Regional variation in returns to education may also be informed by relative regional social and economic development.

a. For more information, see World Development Indicators (database), World Bank, Washington, DC, http://data.worldbank.org/data-catalog/world-development-indicators.

Public Returns to Tertiary Education

Governments subsidize most systems of higher education, and it is possible to measure rates of return of the public cost and benefits accruing to education provision. The calculation of public returns to education takes into account the costs borne by society as a whole (including government spending, individual tuition, and opportunity cost), and the benefits are determined on the basis of pretax earnings instead of posttax earnings. As a consequence, public returns to education measure and assess the efficiency of public spending on education.

In general, public returns to education are smaller than private returns because of the inclusion of public costs. In SSA, the provision of tertiary education is predominantly financed by the state. The intersection of the effects of escalating costs and limited beneficiaries results in a situation in which public returns to education in SSA are dwarfed by private returns for individuals. In comparison, the ratio of private to public returns to tertiary education is much higher than for other regions. Again, in this context, it is worth underlining the fact that a disproportionate share of the public subsidies extended to tertiary education benefits wealthy students. Given these considerations, it is imperative that governments weigh the benefits of returns accruing to higher levels of education against the trade-off incurred with regard to uneducated or less-educated members of society.

Social Returns to Tertiary Education

As the calculation of public rates of return to tertiary education employs observable earnings and costs, the formula considers these benefits quite narrowly. A wider approach considers social rates of return to education, taking into account all the direct benefits and costs associated with investments in education and externalities resulting from the production of education (figure 5.1). The Task Force on Higher Education and Society (2000) argues that research on rates of return to education appraises value accruing to educated people only through higher earnings and improved tax revenues extracted by society. However, the educated pool of citizens benefits society in many different ways.

Figure 5.1 A Classification of Market and Nonmarket Benefits of Education

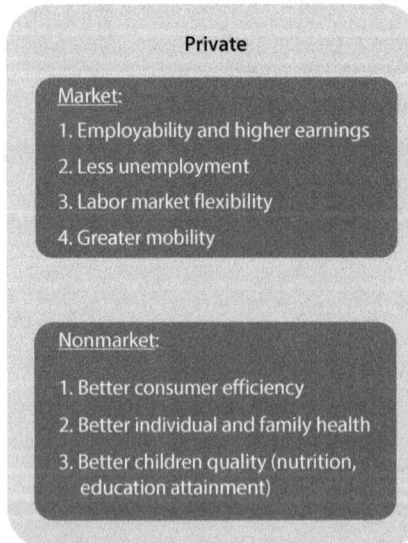
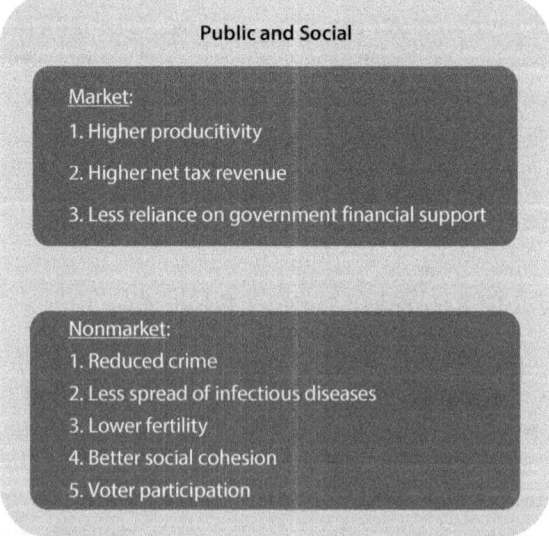

Source: Psacharopoulos 2009.

For example, educated individuals are better positioned to act as economic and social entrepreneurs, with far-reaching implications for the economic and social well-being of their communities. Comparatively well-educated members of society also play a critical role in contributing to environments in which economic development is possible through their role in promoting good governance, staffing and supporting strong institutions, and encouraging and realizing infrastructure development.

On an individual basis, students and families rarely consider the social externalities associated with tertiary education when weighing decisions to pursue tertiary education. This can contribute to an underinvestment in higher levels of education. On a macroeconomic basis, public financing of tertiary education is justified when social returns to tertiary education are higher than private returns.

However, social externalities are difficult to isolate and even more difficult to measure. From a research perspective, there has been significant success in identifying positive externalities associated with education, but few scholars have been able to quantify these externalities (Weisbrod 1964; Haveman and Wolfe 1984). Externalities commonly associated with education include cluster effects, multiplier effects, and entrepreneurial innovation. A *cluster effect* refers to the higher levels of skills and education obtained by individuals who work together because skilled workers raise the productivity of nonskilled workers, resulting in an overall increase in labor productivity. The increase in government tax revenues associated with higher salaries and levels of consumption of more educated individuals is known as the *multiplier effect*. *Entrepreneurial innovation* is strongly associated with the activities of comparatively more-educated workers who are more likely to introduce innovation and drive activities to stimulate market dynamics. The effects of innovation have the potential to stimulate employment creation for less-educated workers and enable an overall economic context characterized by growth, improved competitiveness, and productivity. Notwithstanding the positive effects of these externalities, their value and quantity are difficult to calculate.

Social Mobility and Tertiary Education

The final section of this chapter examines the role played by higher education in increasing the ability of low-income students to move up the income ladder. *Intergenerational mobility* is defined as the situation in which the socioeconomic status of a person is independent of his or her starting conditions (for example, parental or family background). *Intragenerational mobility* refers to the continuum of change in an individual's socioeconomic status through the course of his or her lifetime. In this section we focus primarily on intragenerational mobility.

As discussed above, students from disadvantaged backgrounds are significantly less likely to (be able to) access tertiary education. However, even with tertiary education, social outcomes are not the same for all graduates. Research on the South African labor market demonstrates that the prospects for gaining employment in South Africa are highly dependent on an individual's social networks.

Individuals with a social network of predominantly employed persons have better access to employment opportunities than do individuals from comparatively poor segments of society, who are more likely to have social networks comprising un- or underemployed individuals (Tonheim and Matose 2013).

In the United States, research on students who attend and do not attend a university has demonstrated that the largest benefits accrue to students from underrepresented groups, relative to their non-college-going peers. Brand and Xie (2010) and Dale and Krueger (2011) show that the magnitude of benefits accruing to students who pursue higher education is highest for individuals from the sectors of society least likely to pursue a college education. Students from socially advantaged backgrounds participate in higher education at the highest rate, yet these individuals rely least on tertiary education for access to social status, income, and professional work.

In this section, we compare the returns to tertiary education of students in SSA countries drawn from different income groups using the Heckman selection regression model (Heckman model). In addition to regression analysis and methods used to estimate differences in the private returns to education accruing to these groups, the Heckman model provides a robust analysis that accounts for selection bias.

The results of the Heckman model, illustrated in figure 5.2, demonstrate that in Nigeria and Rwanda the relative income gain for tertiary education graduates is much larger for students from low-income groups than for students from the highest quintiles of income distribution. This suggests that policies that improve the participation of underrepresented groups in tertiary education can more effectively facilitate overall social mobility and prosperity. In Rwanda, tertiary graduates from households in the bottom 40 percent of the income distribution

Figure 5.2 Earning Differences, by Education Level and Income Groups

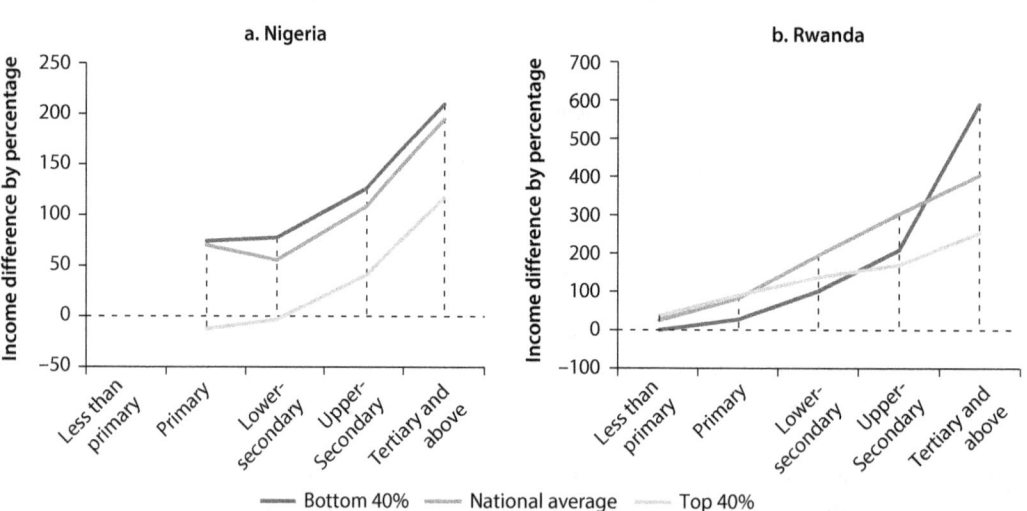

Source: Calculations were made using various years of household survey data.

Figure 5.3 Earning Differences of the Bottom 40 Percent, by Levels of Education

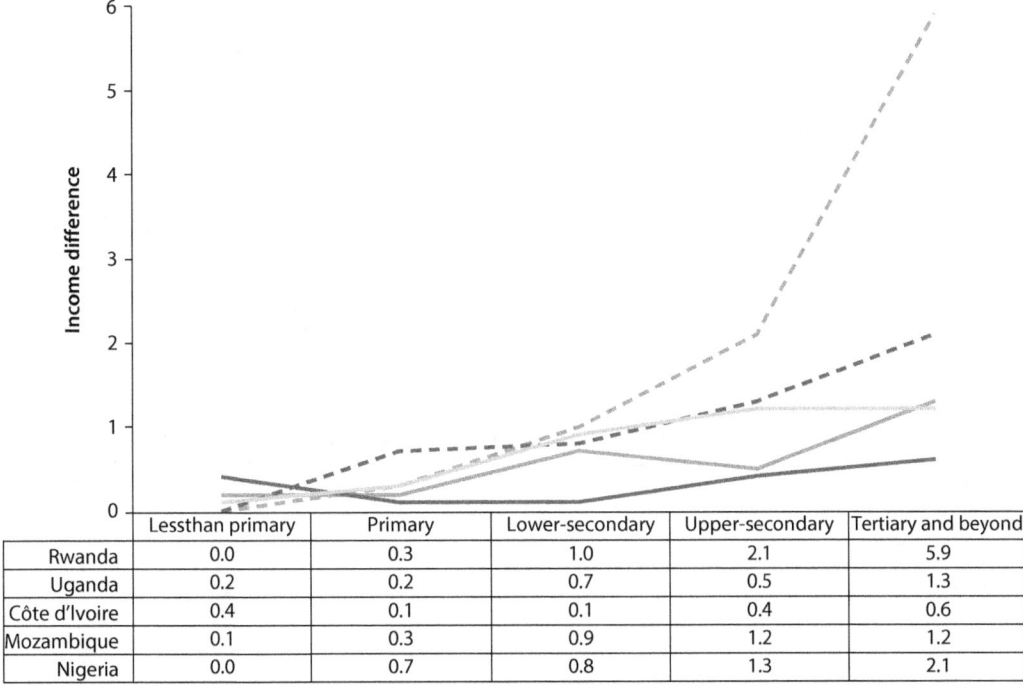

	Less than primary	Primary	Lower-secondary	Upper-secondary	Tertiary and beyond
Rwanda	0.0	0.3	1.0	2.1	5.9
Uganda	0.2	0.2	0.7	0.5	1.3
Côte d'Ivoire	0.4	0.1	0.1	0.4	0.6
Mozambique	0.1	0.3	0.9	1.2	1.2
Nigeria	0.0	0.7	0.8	1.3	2.1

Source: Calculations were made using various years of household survey data.

have earnings 594 percent higher than their socioeconomic peers with no education. By contrast, the equivalent comparison for graduates from households in the highest 40 percent of the income distribution yields an income premium of 255 percent over their less-educated peers. A similar pattern is observed in Nigeria.

As illustrated in figure 5.3, there is significant country-level variance in the magnitude of tertiary education benefits accruing to students from comparatively poor households. For example, much higher returns to tertiary education are observable for students from lower-income quintiles in Rwanda than in Côte d'Ivoire.

References

Brand, J. E., and Y. Xie. 2010. "Who Benefits Most from College? Evidence for Negative Selection in Heterogeneous Economic Returns to Higher Education." *American Sociological Review* 75 (2): 273–302.

Dale, S., and A. B. Krueger. 2011. "Estimating the Return to College Selectivity over the Career Using Administrative Earnings Data." NBER Working Paper 17159, National Bureau of Economic Research, Cambridge, MA.

Darvas, Peter, Marta Favara, Gabriela Munares, and Fei Yuan. 2016. *Skills for Economic Recovery and Shared Growth in the Democratic Republic of Congo.* Washington, DC: World Bank.

Haveman, R. H., and B. Wolfe. 1984. "Schooling and Economic Well-Being: The Role of Non-Market Effects." *Journal of Human Resources* 19 (3): 128–40.

Montenegro, C. E., and H. A. Patrinos. 2014. "Comparable Estimates of Returns to Schooling Around the World." Policy Research Working Paper 7020, World Bank, Washington, DC.

Psacharopoulos, G. 2009. *Returns to Investment in Higher Education: A European Survey.* Higher Education Funding Reform Project, European Commission.

Task Force on Higher Education and Society. 2000. *Higher Education in Developing Countries: Peril and Promise.* Washington, DC: World Bank.

Tonheim, M., and F. Matose. 2013. "South Africa: Social Mobility for a Few?" Norwegian Peacebuilding Resource Centre Report, NOREF, Oslo.

Weisbrod, B. A. 1964. *External Benefits of Public Education: An Economic Analysis.* Princeton, NJ: Princeton University Press.

CHAPTER 6

Government Policies to Address Inequity

Key Messages

- While many countries in Sub-Saharan Africa (SSA) explicitly recognize the role of higher education in reducing poverty, there is a varied degree of alignment between the overall poverty-reduction policy goals of SSA countries and their public expenditures. This alignment can also be associated with their resultant gross enrollment rates for tertiary education.
- Within their respective tertiary institutions, SSA countries have started to include indicators relating to race, socioeconomic background, gender, disability, and region to inform the admissions process and implemented programs to provide more equitable access to traditionally underrepresented groups.
- In the context of increasing cost sharing across SSA countries, well-designed financial aid programs, especially student loan schemes that appropriately target students from low-income households, are key to ensuring and improving equitable access to tertiary institutions.
- In the absence of effective means testing, unsubsidized loans may improve equity more effectively than highly subsidized loan programs. Most SSA countries have poor mechanisms to appraise and recover student loans.
- Private providers of tertiary education follow a diverse range of operating models and vary substantially in quality and scale. They increase the supply of higher education in SSA and contribute to greater access to tertiary education for underrepresented groups. However, their presence does not automatically result in more equitable access or outcomes.
- Governments can extend financial support to private sector students to improve quality and equity.
- Among other innovations, performance-based budgeting and the use of performance indicators linked to equity goals have demonstrated significant utility in improving equity.

The previous chapters established that, despite a significant expansion of the tertiary education sector in SSA, the benefits of this growth disproportionately accrue to students from relatively advantaged households. The persistence of inequity in SSA systems of tertiary education has contributed to a bottleneck in the supply of higher education, which further undermines the region's prospects for catching up with rest of the world. Moreover, the analysis has demonstrated that the magnitude of private returns to tertiary education is highest for students from low-income households, with concurrent and positive effects for improved collective prosperity. As a consequence, there are both short- and long-term effects of government interventions that effectively address inequity in tertiary education by improving access on the part of underserved sections of the population.

This chapter focuses on government policy interventions, targeting specific subpopulations and the interventions' effectiveness in increasing access to tertiary education. To date, the effectiveness of these types of interventions has not been extensively studied.

Country Policy and Institutional Assessment

Improving access to tertiary education is recognized as a key factor contributing to further economic development. As a consequence, in their Poverty Reduction Strategy Papers (PRSPs), many SSA countries have stressed the importance of further developing their systems of tertiary education. Many of these PRSPs focus specifically on expanding access to tertiary education for historically disadvantaged subgroups within the population.

Examples of country priorities drawn from PRSPs in the region are as follows:

- Benin's PRSP underscores the need to improve the quality of education delivered and the need to improve gender equity. To this end, the paper proposes the introduction of scholarships targeting female students to improve their access to university residences.
- Ghana's PRSP notes the critical issues arising as a consequence of persistently limited access to quality tertiary education and the high cost of tertiary education, in a context of significant growth within the youth demographic. The PRSP underscores the need to promote female social empowerment through improved access to education.
- Uganda's PRSP emphasizes the need to improve equitable access to higher education and the need to reduce the impact of the cost of education on families. The PRSP proposes (i) the introduction of a student loan scheme to enable more students to access tertiary education and (ii) a reform of public financing of tertiary education to more effectively target individual students and disciplines (science and technology) rather than institutions.

One way governments can monitor the implementation of policies is through a review of public spending. The World Bank has conducted a series of Country

Policy and Institutional Assessment (CPIA) ratings intended to capture the quality of a country's policies and institutional arrangements. Included in these studies is an indicator to assess the equity of public resource use, which measures the extent to which patterns of public expenditures and revenue collection affect the poor and the extent to which these patterns are consistent with national poverty reduction priorities. Although one cannot effectively determine causality between the relative equity of public resource use and a country's level of tertiary enrollment, the data do provide country-specific insights.

Countries in the upper-right quadrant of figure 6.1—such as Benin, Ghana, Nigeria, and Uganda—have a more effective alignment of public expenditures with poverty reduction goals, and are concurrently achieving relatively high rates of enrollment in tertiary education. Countries in the lower-left quadrant—such as the Central African Republic, Chad, and Côte d'Ivoire—are considered to have relatively poor alignment of public expenditures with poverty reduction goals and have low rates of enrollment in tertiary education.

Gender equality is used to assess the extent to which a country has been successful in promoting institutions, laws, and programs to promote equal access for male and female students in education, systems of health, the economy, and protection under the law. The larger the CPIA gender equality value for a country, the more gender sensitive its policies are considered to be. Higher levels of

Figure 6.1 Equity of Public Resource Use and Tertiary Enrollment per 100,000 Inhabitants

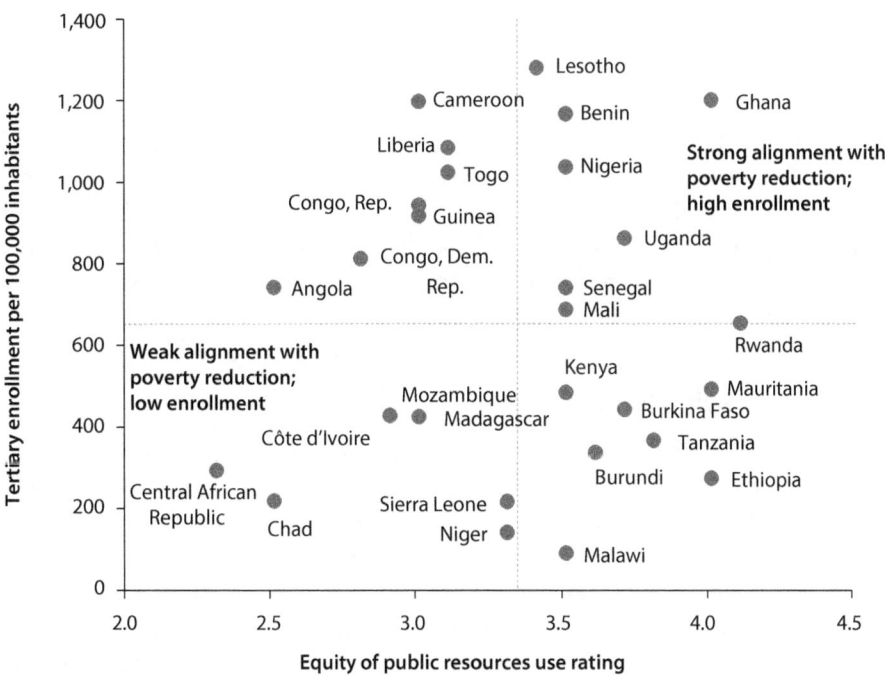

Source: World Bank CPIA data.
Note: Data are from the most recent year available.

Figure 6.2 Country Policy and Institutional Assessment on Gender Equality and Tertiary Enrollment per 100,000 Inhabitants

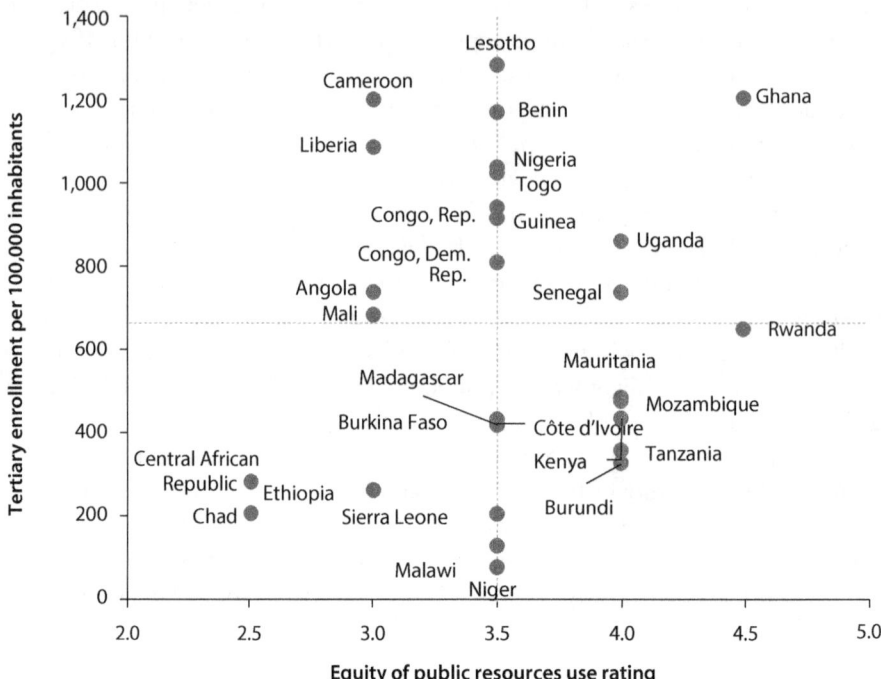

Source: World Bank CPIA data and calculations were made, using household survey data.
Note: Data are from the most recent year available. CPIA = Country Policy and Institutional Assessment.

gender equality are associated with improved female enrollment in tertiary education. In figure 6.2, the countries in the upper-right quadrant—including Ghana, Senegal, and Uganda—have relatively well-established gender programs and relatively high overall tertiary enrollment. Countries in the bottom-left quadrant—such as Central African Republic and Chad—however, demonstrate low levels of tertiary enrollment and are assessed to have relatively ineffective or absent interventions to promote gender equality.

Admissions Policy Initiatives

In an effort to further promote equity in access to tertiary education, a number of countries have included indicators relating to race, socioeconomic background, gender, disability, and region to inform the admissions process. For example, in Uganda, the admissions system reserves 25 percent of 4,000 government-supported positions in higher education for the purposes of addressing equity. This policy is implemented through a quota system to select the best students in each district and to promote the inclusion of students with disabilities and male and female athletes who meet the minimum requirements for specific institutions and programs (Wanyama 2015). In Ghana, the Kwame Nkrumah University of Science and Technology pioneered a quota-based admission system that allows students from underprivileged schools (that are categorized by the Ghana Education Service as less-endowed schools) to enroll as long as they have met the basic entry qualifications (Morley et al. 2007). In Ghana, Kenya, Nigeria, Tanzania, Uganda, and Zimbabwe, either the academic threshold for female entry has been lowered or female applicants are assigned bonus points when taking admissions exams (Morley 2006). At the University of Cape Coast in Ghana, the Joint Admissions Board has targeted female enrollment of 35 percent (or above) of total enrollment (Morley et al. 2007). Although the introduction of affirmative action programs has been controversial in some instances, research suggests that some of these programs are successfully changing the participation patterns of female students—for example, in the bachelor of science in engineering program at the University of Dar es Salaam (Morley et al. 2007). However, it should also be noted that these students may be placed into less-demanded programs as institutions maximize space for fee-paying students in the best programs. This ultimately works against the objective of ensuring equitable outcomes from tertiary education (Liang 2002).

Bridge Programs

To ensure that all students have an equal opportunity to compete for entry into tertiary education, efforts to improve equity in tertiary education need to be initiated in pre-tertiary cycles of education, particularly in primary and secondary education (Salmi et al. 2002). A number of SSA countries have initiated outreach and bridge programs between the tertiary sector and secondary schools, have established special programs and initiatives to target underprivileged groups, and have reformed curricula to improve completion rates.

In South Africa, for example, several programs exist to more effectively prepare secondary school students from disadvantaged communities for entry into tertiary education. These include the Mathematics and Science Exam Preparations Project; Mathematics Incubator Schools for Science, Technology, Engineering, and Mathematics (STEM) at the Nelson Mandela Metropolitan University; and the Siyabona Program, which assists students who demonstrate a strong interest in pursuing commerce at the tertiary level (Blunt 2000). In Namibia, the Pathways Program at the University of Namibia targets students from the marginalized Ovambo ethnic group, with a focus on improved preparation for the study of tertiary level sciences and engineering (MacGregor 2008).

Research suggests that improving the flow of information relating to technology, job opportunities, and returns to different types of employment can be effective and relatively inexpensive interventions to aid improved decision making on the part of would-be applicants to higher education, particularly female applicants. This can be done relatively easily and cost-effectively through the use of mass media, such as radio, television, newspaper, and the Internet (Hino and Ranis 2014).

Financial Aid

In a context of increasing the adoption of cost-sharing initiatives to fund tertiary education, governments must improve the design and delivery of financial aid programs and focus on protecting relatively underprivileged students from the exclusionary effects associated with levying private costs. Low-income students who receive financial aid are more likely to remain in higher education and graduate (Rowan-Kenyon et al. 2009). In most countries, the introduction of tuition fees has been preceded, or quickly followed, by the development of financial aid programs and/or the introduction of student loan schemes. The extent to which SSA governments are successful in providing financial support to students in need depends on the degree to which grants and loans are effectively designed, targeted, distributed, and recovered.

Financial aid in, the form of need-based grants and scholarships, is an effective but expensive means for expanding participation and addressing equity gaps. Salmi and Hauptman (2006) argue that the allocation of funds directly to students is a more effective method for increasing participation on the part of traditionally underserved groups than allocating these funds to public tertiary institutions. They note that input-based budgets at universities do not necessarily differentiate between inputs (students) on the basis of gender, ethnicity, socioeconomic status, and so on.

The effective administration of need-based grants requires efficient and transparent targeting mechanisms. Means testing on the basis of household income is a contentious and complicated issue in SSA, in part because of the large share of the labor force employed in the informal sector and the resulting unreliability of earnings data. As a consequence, some researchers argue for the introduction of proxy indicators of relative wealth, such as home ownership, rather than a sole reliance on income indicators for means testing (Tekleselassie and Johnstone 2004).

Governments are increasingly using student loan schemes to reduce the overall cost of administering financial aid (table 6.1). Johnstone and Marcucci (2010) argue that the improved provision of loans not only expands access to education but also reduces historically regressive patterns of public resource distribution in education, in part because beneficiaries of loans for tertiary education are obliged to pay back these loans. Similarly, the Global University Network for Innovation (GUNI 2006) has argued that student loan schemes promote equity because they allow students from low-income households to borrow money to pay for an education they would not otherwise have been able to afford, and to repay when they can. Shen and Ziderman (2009) estimate that government-sponsored student loan schemes are in place in 70 countries worldwide and that this number is growing quickly.

In general, African countries have performed poorly in the appraisal and recovery of student loans. Low rates of student loan recovery constitute a significant sustainability risk for government loan programs. The efficiency of student loans as a means for promoting improved access to tertiary education is

Table 6.1 Student Loan Schemes in Sub-Saharan Africa

Country	Origination	Eligibility	Means Tested	Cosignatories	Contingent on Income	Capital Provision
Botswana	Dept. of Tert. Ed. Fin. (gov.)	General availability	No	No		Government
Burkina Faso	Government	General availability	Yes	No		Government
Ethiopia	Universities	General availability	No	No		Government
Ghana	Student Loan Trust Fund	General availability	Yes	Yes		Pension fund (SSNIT)
Kenya	Higher Education Loans Board	General availability	Yes	Yes		Government
Nigeria	Nigerian Education Bank	General availability	No	No		Government
South Africa	Tertiary Ed. Fund for South Africa (TEFSA)	General availability	Yes	No		Government
South Africa (Knight 2009)	National Student Financial Aid Scheme (NSFAS)				Yes	Government
Tanzania	Government	General availability	Yes	No		Government

Source: International Comparative Higher Education Finance and Accessibility Project, http://www.gse.buffalo.edu/org/IntHigherEdFinance.

compromised by, among other things, low interest rates, unnecessarily long repayment periods, poor information on the part of graduates about repayment schedules, generous default policies, poor recordkeeping, and the high cost of loan recovery (Experton and Fevre 2010). Improving the design, repayment monitoring, and enforcement of loan recovery programs will be critical for improving the sustainability of government-supported loan programs.

Low recovery and interest rates mean that virtually all student loan programs in SSA require some form of public subsidization. In weighing the benefits of schemes, the cost to the taxpayer of subsidizing student loan schemes—including all publicly funded subsidies, administrative costs, and default guarantees—must be assessed in relation to the costs and benefits associated with other schemes, such as free or highly subsidized tuition or need-based grants (Johnstone 2004).

In the absence of effective means testing, unsubsidized loans may improve equity more effectively than highly subsidized loan programs. Salmi and Hauptman (2006) demonstrate that student loan schemes tend to disproportionately benefit students from upper- and middle-income households in the absence of effective means testing. Moreover, because highly subsidized loan programs are more expensive for governments to finance, fewer students will be in a position to access funds than with loan schemes at lower subsidies.

Castañeda et al. (2005) identify numerous factors that require consideration in designing a student loan scheme. These include the need to ensure (i) an appropriate data collection strategy, (ii) adequate and effective management, (iii) the feasibility and accuracy of verification mechanisms, (iv) institutional arrangements, and (v) effective monitoring and oversight mechanisms to ensure transparency, credibility, and fraud prevention.

Income-contingent loans require the repayment of a loan based on the borrower's income. Although income-contingent loans have the potential to improve equity by linking labor market outcomes to the burden of payment, they are difficult to implement and monitor, which can compromise loan recovery. In low-income countries, which are characterized by underdeveloped tax systems and significant informal sector economic activity, the proportion of taxpayers as a share of the total population averages only 5 percent, whereas that proportion is 46 percent in developed countries (Zolt and Bird 2005). Moreover, in many low-income countries it is extremely difficult to obtain accurate and reliable data regarding the salaries of graduates and therefore to calculate a borrower's monthly payments.

Diversification

The development of private universities increases the chances that students from disadvantaged backgrounds will access tertiary education. Students from disadvantaged households tend to be less prepared than their peers from comparatively wealthy households to meet the admission requirements for access to public universities. As a consequence, despite the fact that private universities are more likely to charge various fees for tertiary education, their admissions policies do not exacerbate inequity in tertiary education. However, the presence of private universities does not automatically lend itself to improved equity. Carrol (2005) compares the socioeconomic status of students admitted to Uganda's Makerere University under the Private Entry Scheme (PES) to those admitted through the government scholarship scheme and demonstrates that the PES has entrenched, rather than increased, existing inequities in participation at the university.

Private tertiary education providers are diverse, and include for-profit companies, not-for-profit institutions, religious institutions, foreign private universities, and others. As a consequence, the quality of education provision in private higher education institutions (HEIs) is variable. Private institutions serving comparatively poor students are usually set up in converted buildings. In many African countries, private HEIs often operate as unlicensed institutions (Bjarnason et al. 2008). Other private universities have proven to be innovative in driving curriculum reform and encouraging critical thinking, and in so doing have established reputations as centers of excellence. An example is Ashesi University College in Ghana, a not-for-profit university established by a former Microsoft engineer.

Effective regulation of private higher education provision is necessary to ensure quality. Theoretically, labor market forces (future employment) should eliminate poor or substandard education providers. However, in the absence of reliable information on labor market outcomes, ensuring the maintenance of standards and equitable outcomes in the private institutions requires regulation. However, the regulation of private university licenses should also be predictable and efficient so as not to discourage private investment in this sector.

Some countries, such as Ghana, limit, or attempt to limit, tuition fees charged by private HEIs. This may have unintended consequences (Bjarnason et al. 2008). While such a policy aims to ensure access to private tertiary education for a wider group of students, it may not recognize the fact that many private universities depend entirely on student tuition to cover operational costs. Capping tuition fees may therefore discourage private HEIs from expanding operations. An alternative policy is for governments to extend financial support to private sector students. This can help expand access to private higher education and promote equity goals.

Moreover, the unit cost of private sector tertiary education is, in some cases, lower than unit costs in the public system. In these contexts, it is cost effective for the government to encourage students to opt for training in the private sector, even if this requires some form of financial support for students (Gioan 2008). Subsidizing private HEI also enables the state to impose requirements, particularly with regard to quality, teaching conditions, and results. The provision of financial support to the private higher education sector, through tax incentives or direct student sponsorship, can potentially reduce fees and improve participation on the part of students from disadvantaged households.

In many African university systems, access is limited to the best-performing secondary school graduates, who come disproportionately from the wealthiest households. Nonuniversity institutions benefit students from low-performing secondary schools who do not qualify for admission to public tertiary universities. However, students who enroll in nonuniversity and short-cycle educational institutions do not necessarily continue with further higher education.

In SSA, the academic path to a university education is often rigid, and course articulation and credit-transfer mechanisms that allow students to move between different levels of education and different types of institutions are rarely institutionalized. Staff and student mobility between university and nonuniversity tertiary institutions is undermined by poor cooperation and an absence of dialogue between institutional groups. In the admissions process, some universities do not recognize any credits or skills acquired through study at a polytechnic institution. The mobility of students between private and public universities and between public universities is rare, particularly in Anglophone Africa (Ng'ethe, Subotzky, and Afeti 2008). However, in Francophone countries, such as Cameroon and Senegal, HEIs that deliver subdegree polytechnic qualifications are linked to universities and are not seen as entirely separate or autonomous institutions (Ng'ethe, Subotzky, and Afeti 2008). The Kigali Institute of Science and Technology in Rwanda, for example, has created a cumulative system of credit, comprising four levels that cumulatively accrue toward a degree qualification (Ng'ethe et al. 2003).

Budget Management

In making decisions to finance systems of tertiary education, governments need to balance equity goals with the availability of government financing. Expanding access to tertiary education for disadvantaged students can pose public finance challenges, as demonstrated by post-apartheid South Africa. In the aftermath of apartheid, the number of black students admitted to tertiary education increased rapidly, but the government lacked adequate funding for them (Badsha and Wickham 2013).

Tax revenues are invariably the cheapest source of funding for education; however, in African countries it is not easy to expand the tax base. On average, in recent years, public revenue in low-income SSA countries has been equivalent to 18 percent of gross domestic product (GDP), compared with 29 percent in middle-income SSA countries. The International Monetary Fund estimates that many low-income countries could attain an increase in tax revenues of about 4 percent of GDP (OECD 2014). Systems that include generous tax exemptions, in combination with high rates of tax evasion on the part of wealthy and corporate elites, significantly inhibit effective revenue collection in SSA. In Burundi, for example, tax exemptions in 2012 were estimated at US$70 million, equivalent to 3 percent of GDP, or approximately one-fifth of total revenue (World Bank 2013). Similarly, overly complex tax systems, and the limited number of skilled personnel to oversee tax collection, impede efficient tax collection. In Equatorial Guinea, weak tax administration and an inefficient institutional design (several bodies participate in revenue administration) undermine efforts on the part of government to expand the tax base (World Bank 2012).

Improving domestic revenue mobilization will require that governments address regressive and inequitable tax policies, improve transparency, and significantly invest in enabling information technology infrastructure. These are all structural challenges and require medium- to long-term reform horizons. As a consequence, it is unlikely that many countries in SSA will be in a position to sustainably address the growing demand for tertiary education through an increase in domestic revenues in the short to medium terms.

Innovative Financing for Higher Education

Performance-based budgeting and the use of performance indicators linked to equity goals have demonstrated significant utility in improving equity. Performance measurements can include internal *efficiency indicators*, such as graduation and retention rates, and *equity indicators*, such as the share of female enrollment as a proportion of total enrollment and the equivalent share of students from disadvantaged households. Although, as of 2013, no African country had implemented a fully fledged performance- and program-based budgeting (PPBB) system, over 80 percent of SSA countries have experimented with, or are committed to introducing, some form of PPBB (CABRI 2013). In most countries, PPBB systems are being implemented as part of the larger public financial management reform initiatives, or are driven by an increased interest in output- or performance-based aid and donor activities.

Examples from developed countries in which private capital has been leveraged to finance systems of tertiary education may be transferable to developing countries. Positive examples include the issuing of bonds, the securitization of student loans, encouraging investment in private institutions on the part of private equity firms in anticipation of future profits, and long-term partnerships with the philanthropy sector (Hahn 2007).

In SSA, the market potential of tertiary education is often insufficient to encourage greater participation by private actors. Although the demand for innovative financial products in support of tertiary students and institutions is high, commercial banks and private sector investors to date have only tentatively tested these products and interventions. As a consequence, the policy and regulatory environment must play a crucial role in facilitating the leveraging of private capital and associated benefits in the service of tertiary education provision—for example, through government enforcement of loan repayments. Other mechanisms could include government-facilitated public-private partnerships, the adoption of appropriate tax codes, and improved collection of income-related data for more effective means testing (Hahn 2007).

References

Badsha, N., and S. Wickham. 2013. *Review of Initiatives in Equity and Transformation in Three Universities in South Africa*. Wynberg, South Africa: Cape Higher Education Consortium (CHEC).

Bjarnason, S., H. A. Patrinos, J.-P. Tan, J. Fielden, and N. Larocque. 2008. "The Evolving Regulatory Context for Private Education in Emerging Economies." Working Paper 154, World Bank, Washington, DC.

Blunt, R. 2000. "Issues in School to College Transition in Developing Countries: The Case of South Africa." Paper presented at the annual meeting of the Association for the Study of Higher Education.

CABRI (Collaborative African Budget Reform Initiative). 2013. *Performance and Programme-Based Budgeting in Africa: A Status Report*. Pretoria: CABRI Secretariat.

Carrol, B. 2005. *Private Monies, Public Universities: Implications for Access and University Behavior—A Study of Makerere University (Uganda)*. Stanford, CA: Stanford University Press.

Castañeda, T., K. Lindert, B. de la Briere, L. Fernandez, C. Hubert, O. Larranaya. M. Orozco, and R. Viquez. 2005. "Designing and Implementing Household Targeting Systems: Lessons from Latin America and the United States." Social Protection Discussion Paper 526, World Bank, Washington, DC.

Experton, William, and Chloe Fevre. 2010. *Financing Higher Education in Africa*. Directions in Development Series. Washington, DC: World Bank.

Gioan, A. P. 2008. *Higher Education in Francophone Africa: What Tools Can Be Used to Support Financially-Sustainable Policies?* Washington, DC: World Bank.

Hahn, R. 2007. *The Global State of Higher Education and the Rise of Private Finance*. Washington, DC: Institute for Higher Education Policy, Global Centre for Private Financing of Higher Education.

Hino, H., and G. Ranis. 2014. *Youth and Employment in Sub-Saharan Africa: Working but Poor*. New York: Routledge.

Johnstone, D. B. 2004. "Cost-Sharing and Equity in Higher Education: Implications of Income Contingent Loans." *Higher Education Dynamics* 6: 37–59.

Johnstone, D. B., and P. Marcucci. 2010. *Financially Sustainable Student Loan Programs: The Management of Risk in the Quest for Private Capital*. Washington, DC: Institute for Higher Educational Policy, Global Center on the Private Financing of Higher Education.

Knight, Jane, ed. 2009. *Financing Access and Equity in Higher Education*. Rotterdam: Sense Publishers.

Liang, Xiaovang. 2004. "Uganda Post-Primary Education Sector Report." Africa Region Human Development Working Paper 30, World Bank, Washington, DC.

MacGregor, K. 2008. *Case Study: Namibia—University of Namibia*. Pathways to Higher Education: A Ford Foundation Global Initiative for Promoting Inclusiveness in Higher Education.

GUNI (Global University Network for Innovation). 2006. *Higher Education in the World 2006: The Financing of Universities*. London: Palgrave Macmillan UK.

Morley, L. 2006. *Gender Equity in Commonwealth Higher Education: An Examination of Sustainable Interventions in Selected Commonwealth Universities*. London: U.K. Department for International Development.

Morley, L., F. Leach, R. Lugg, E. Bhalalusesa, R. Mwaipopo, L. Dzama Forde, and G. Egbanya. 2007. *Widening Participation in Higher Education in Ghana and Tanzania: Developing an Equity Scorecard*. Brighton: University of Sussex (U.K.) Centre for Higher Education & Equity.

Ng'ethe, N., N. Assie-Lumumba, G. Subotzky, and E. Sutheland-Addy. 2003. *Higher Education Innovations in Sub-Saharan Africa: With Specific Reference to Universities*. Accra: Association of African Universities.

Ng'ethe, N., G. Subotzky, and G. Afeti. 2008. *Differentiation and Articulation in Tertiary Education Systems: A Study of Twelve African Countries*. Washington, DC: World Bank.

OECD (Organisation for Economic Co-operation and Development). 2014. *Development Co-operation Report 2014: Mobilising Resources for Sustainable Development*. Paris: OECD Publishing.

Rowan-Kenyon, H., R. Blanchard, B. Reed, and A. Swan. 2009. "Social and Cultural Predictors of Low-SES Student Persistence in College." Association for the Study of Higher Education Conference, Vancouver.

Salmi, J., and A. M. Hauptman. 2006. *Innovations in Tertiary Education Financing: A Comparative Evaluation of Allocation Mechanisms*. Washington, DC: World Bank.

Salmi, J., B. Millot, D. Court, M. Crawford, P. Darvas, F. Golladay, L. Holm-Nielsen, R. Hopper, A. Markov, P. Moock, H. Mukherjee, W. Saint, S. Shrivastava, F. Steier, and R. van Meel. 2002. *Constructing Knowledge Societies*. Directions in Development Series. Washington, DC: World Bank.

Shen, H., and A. Ziderman. 2009. "Student Loans: Repayment and Recovery: International Comparisons." *Higher Education* 57: 315–33.

Tekleselassie, A., and D. B. Johnstone. 2004. "Means Testing: The Dilemma of Targeting Subsidies in African Higher Education." *Journal of Higher Education in Africa* 2 (2): 135–58.

Wanyama, Michael O. 2015. "Loan Scheme Will Increase Access to Higher Education for Needy." *Daily Monitor*, June 23.

World Bank. 2012. *Equatorial Guinea: Public Expenditure Review*. Washington, DC: World Bank.

———. 2013. *Burundi—Public Expenditure Review: Strengthening Fiscal Resilience to Promote Government Effectiveness*. Washington, DC: World Bank.

Zolt, E. M., and R. M. Bird. 2005. *Redistribution via Taxation: The Limited Role of the Personal Income Tax in Development Countries*. Los Angeles: University of California, Los Angeles, School of Law.

CHAPTER 7

In-Depth Country Case Studies

Introduction

This chapter presents 10 country cases that demonstrate how tertiary education policies affect outcomes and patterns of equity in Sub-Saharan Africa (SSA). The selection of country case studies is based on the availability of data, including the extensive analysis of financing tertiary education published by the World Bank. Table 7.1 summarizes a number of tertiary education indicators that have been discussed throughout this book for our 10 case study countries.

The Case of Ghana

Ghana's tertiary education sector is one of SSA's success stories. Education spending in Ghana was equivalent to 8.1 percent of the country's gross domestic product (GDP) in 2011. Of the total spending on education, approximately 13 percent is dedicated to tertiary education; and, from a regional perspective, the country demonstrates relatively high enrollment rates in tertiary education. Although it is true that the richest segment of the population disproportionately benefits from access to tertiary education, Ghana is one of the few countries in the region wherein students from households in the bottom quintiles of income distribution represent a respectable share of tertiary enrollment. The gender parity index, however, is below the SSA average. The ratio of per-tertiary-student spending to per-primary-student spending is reasonable, at 3.9.

Socioeconomic status remains the largest determinant of a student's chance of accessing a university education in Ghana. A benefit incidence analysis demonstrates that students from the highest quintile of income distribution accrue 47 percent of the benefits associated with the government's subsidy of tertiary education, in comparison to the 5 percent accruing to the bottom quintile (figure 7.1). Disparities in tertiary education are representative of accumulated inequity in pre-tertiary levels of education. Students from comparatively wealthy households are more likely to attend private

Table 7.1 Tertiary Education Indicators in Selected SSA Countries

Indicator	Ghana	Guinea	Kenya	Malawi	Mozambique	Niger	Nigeria	Senegal	Sierra Leone	Uganda
Enrollment in tertiary education per 100,000 inhabitants, both sexes	1,370	931.9	422	79	496	126.9	997	711.2	600	399
Gross enrollment ratio, gender parity index, tertiary	0.63	0.44	0.7	0.65	0.69	0.34	0.72	0.59	0.79	0.78
Gross enrollment ratio, postsecondary, bottom 40 percent	1.38	—	1.32	0	0	4.3	1.57	13.2	0	3.32
Gross enrollment ratio, postsecondary, richest quintile	12.75	—	10.42	5.92	5.61	47	20.22	19.3	8.9	11.78
Ratio of per-tertiary-student cost over per-primary-student cost	3.9	13.1	11.4	224.5	12	—	—	—	—	12.3

Source: World Bank EdStats.
Note: SSA = Sub-Saharan Africa." — = not available."

Figure 7.1 Benefit Incidence at Different Levels of Education

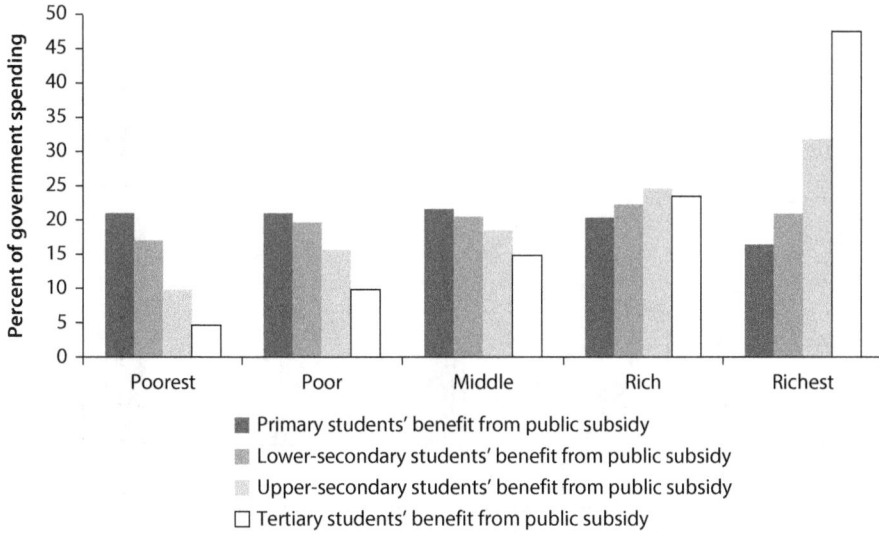

Source: Calculations are based on a household survey.

schools and benefit from high-quality teaching, and they are more likely to hire private tutors to prepare them for higher education. A household in the top quintile of household income spends on average 11 times more money for one child to attend primary and lower-secondary school than does a household located in the bottom quintile of income distribution (figure 7.2). The equivalent measures for upper-secondary and tertiary education are 3.8 and 3, respectively.

In 1997, Ghana made cost sharing in tertiary education mandatory through the adoption of the Akosombo Accord. Under the current system, 70 percent of total university funding comes from government resources, with the remaining 30 percent sourced from internally generated revenues, tuition fees, and private donations. Of the latter three sources of revenue, income derived from tuition fees makes up the largest share of nonpublic funding. Originally, it was intended that tuition fees would be levied only on international students, who would make up no more than 10 percent of enrollment. However, when international enrollment failed to meet the 10 percent threshold, institutions were permitted to fill their quota by levying fees on Ghanaian students who would otherwise not have gained entrance to universities. In practice, Ghana's system is broadly aligned with the "dual-track" practices common in many other African and Eastern European systems of higher education (Marcucci 2007).

In 2007, Ghana established the Student Loan Trust Fund (SLTF), which makes loans on the basis of means testing and program differentiation available to students. Commendably, loans dispersed under the auspices of SLTF are

Figure 7.2 Average Household Spending on Education, by Income Quintile

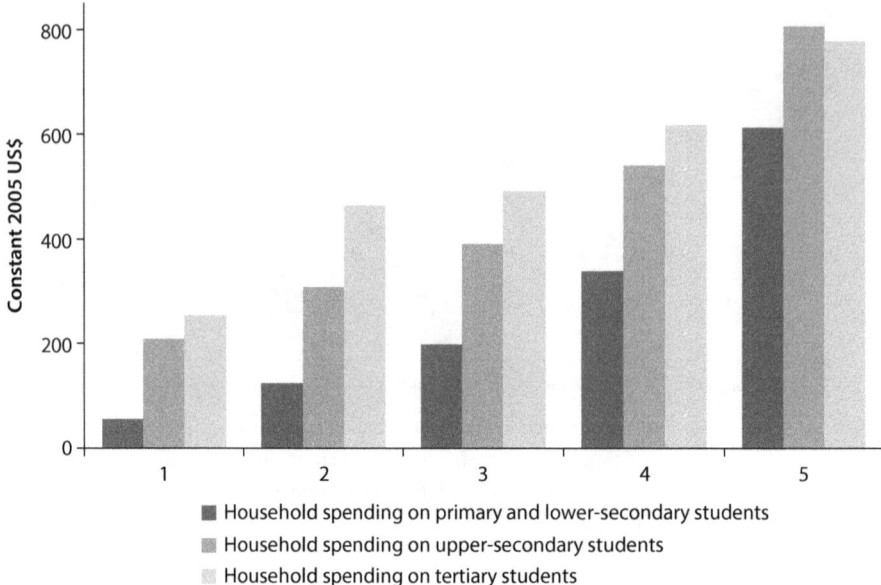

- Household spending on primary and lower-secondary students
- Household spending on upper-secondary students
- Household spending on tertiary students

Source: Calculations are based on a household survey.

subject to real interest rates, minimizing potential government losses associated with inflation, loan administration, and loan default. The SLTF loan program is, however, hamstrung by delays in the distribution of loans to students; and, because schools require the payment of tuition fees prior to the commencement of the academic year, these delays have a disproportionate impact on students from disadvantaged groups.

The government of Ghana has addressed admissions practices in an effort to improve equity in tertiary education. In 2005, the government replaced the system whereby senior staff at universities selected upper-secondary students for admission to tertiary education with a Computerized School Selection and Placement System. The current system perpetuates discrimination against students from rural areas because it privileges student scores from exams, which in turn are disproportionately informed by the quality of schooling a student receives and the fact that the majority of high-performing schools in the country are located in urban areas (Anyan 2011). The Less-Endowed Schools (LES) Initiative classifies disadvantaged secondary schools in each district on the basis of indicators including the local poverty rate, the turnover of teachers, and relative accessibility. In turn, the Kwame Nkrumah University of Science and Technology has pioneered a quota-based admissions system that allows students from schools classified as LES, who have met the basic qualifications for entry, to enroll even if they have not met the competitive cut-off point required for entry to various programs. The University of Ghana and the University of Cape Coast have replicated this initiative (Morley et al. 2007). Moreover, female applicants to the University of Ghana are admitted with scores one point lower than those of their male counterparts, and the University for Development Studies admits all female applicants who meet the basic qualifications for entry.

The Case of Guinea

The government of Guinea launched an education sector reform plan in 2007 that focused on addressing disparities and on improving teaching and learning outcomes. The education plan set goals for increasing coverage and retention, improving the quality of learning at all levels of education, and diversifying the supply of education. Specific targets were set for 2015, including that tertiary education develop programs with the capacity and quality to meet the needs of the Guinean economy; improve investment in infrastructure; and increase spending per student. However, the interventions associated with these objectives were not successfully implemented.

Guinea's population is very young and growing rapidly, particularly in urban areas. The proportion of the population of school-going age is approximately half the total population of the country, and the size of the generational cohort aligned with secondary school is growing faster than the general population, at 3.3–3.4 percent. Between 1998 and 2011, primary school enrollment more than doubled (from approximately 74,000 to more than 1.6 million students), and secondary school enrollment quadrupled (from approximately 154,000 to over 650,000). Over the same period, the share of enrollment in private education increased rapidly across all levels of education.

Guinea demonstrates high levels of disparity throughout its education system. Gender, location, and socioeconomic dynamics serve as mutually reinforcing factors that exacerbate disparities in access and performance. Enrollment rates for children from poor households fall far below the national average—even at the primary level, where education is ostensibly compulsory. Poor and rural children are more likely to repeat a grade and drop out, are less likely to transition to higher grades, and are more likely to attend schools characterized by suboptimal learning outcomes and poor infrastructure. Outside of Conakry, the capital city, 40 percent of children between 6 and 10 years of age are out of school. The average out-of-school rate for children and youth (age 7–20) is 53 percent (inclusive of individuals who never enrolled in school and those who dropped out); however, for individuals of equivalent ages from the highest quintile of income, this rate is only 20 percent. Half of youth and children from households engaged primarily in agriculture are out of school, compared with only 1 in 10 children from households engaged in economic activities relating to government, health, and education.

In Guinea, the social distribution of costs associated with education are regressive. The average Guinean household spends approximately 13 percent of its disposable income on education; however, the share of disposable income dedicated to education among poorer households is much higher.

Higher education in Guinea is disproportionately concentrated in the capital, with 65 percent of all students enrolled in the sector located in Conakry. Male students account for three-quarters of total enrollment in higher education.

In 2012, public spending on education in Guinea was equivalent to approximately 2.6 percent of GDP, down from 4.4 percent in 2010 and 3.1 percent in 2011. The years 2009 and 2010 coincided with the transition government and were characterized by profligate spending across many sectors. This spending should therefore not be interpreted as being representative of a particular commitment to expanding investment in the education sector.

The tertiary sector in Guinea accounts for 8 percent of the total population of students enrolled in education in the country but benefits from one-third of total public expenditures in the sector. University students, in both public and private institutions, receive scholarships or tuition assistance from the government. In 2012, the Guinean government allocated GF 175 billion to support expenses associated with the provision of scholarships and direct transfers to students in higher education, accounting for half of current expenditures associated with higher education. Higher education also receives the largest share of the total allocation of capital expenditures extended to the education sector. The subsidization of higher education through scholarships and other transfers to students is perceived as an entitlement program that benefits students and universities; as a consequence, reforming the current system will be politically very difficult, despite its relative inefficiency (World Bank 2015).

The Case of Kenya

In 2010, the government of Kenya allocated the equivalent of 5.5 percent of GDP to spending on education, with 15 percent of total education spending assigned to higher education. Kenya has achieved relatively high gross enrollment ratios (GERs) in primary and secondary school, at 114 and 67 percent, respectively. Enrollment in tertiary education stands at 422 students per 100,000 inhabitants. The gender equity index for tertiary enrollment is 0.7, approximately equivalent to the average for SSA.

Kenya introduced a dual-track admissions policy for tertiary education in 1998. The current system admits a restricted number of students to higher education on the basis of merit and at very low cost (because of the public subsidy extended to these students), with the remaining applicants admitted on a fee-paying basis. In private universities, fees are charged on the basis of full cost recovery, in alignment with market forces (Ngome 2003).

The majority of students admitted to public universities as regular students attended high-quality secondary schools, which in turn increasingly admit pupils from comparatively expensive private primary schools. Students from private schools perform, on average, better than students from public schools on national achievement tests toward the Kenya Certificate of Primary Education (KCPE) and Kenya Certificate of Secondary Education (KCSE) (Amburo 2011). The associated equity concerns arising from this disparity have led the government to consider introducing a quota system to limit the number of students admitted to universities from private schools, a decision that has received overwhelming support (Mulongo 2013).

Enrollment of female students is higher in private universities than in public universities. The comparatively high enrollment of female students in private universities is in turn a reflection of the relative performance of male and female secondary students on the KCSE and the smaller pool of female students who meet the cut-off points for admission to public universities. Patterns of admission, moreover, are aligned with regional disparities. According to the Development Policy Management Forum (DPMF 2012), patterns of access to education in Kenya continue to perpetuate the colonial development policies that resulted in certain regions receiving disproportional benefits.

The government created the Higher Education Loans Board (HELB) to administer means-tested loans that support students enrolled in both public and private universities. HELB prioritizes support for students on the basis of means-tested need, students who are orphaned because of HIV/AIDS, and students from regions classified as disadvantaged. However, in practice, HELB does not have the capacity to effectively measure household income, with one study estimating that approximately 25 percent of loan recipients lied about the education, employment, and income status of their parents (Mwiria and Ng'ethe 2002).

Although students enrolled in private universities are eligible for HELB-administered loans, the value of these loans is generally insufficient to cover costs. Tuition in private universities can be as much as 11 times higher than that levied in public universities. HELB cannot increase the value of loans to support the cost of tuition in private universities without triggering demands on the part of public universities for increased tuition fees (Otieno 2004).

The Case of Malawi

Although the tertiary education system in Malawi remains relatively small, participation in tertiary education has steadily increased. In 2011, there were only 79 tertiary students per 100,000 inhabitants, significantly below the SSA average. Persistently low enrollment in tertiary education is in part a consequence of low enrollment in secondary education, where the GER is only 15 percent. Poverty contributes significantly to low levels of participation in secondary school because of public secondary schools' practice of charging fees (Hall and Mambo 2015). Moreover, net admission to the University of Malawi is limited to the number of seats and beds available at the university. As a consequence, the university admits only 1,000 new students each year, and many qualified candidates are turned away.

From an equity perspective, Malawi's education system faces significant challenges. Fifty-four percent of the government subsidy supporting primary education benefits students from the two poorest quintiles of income distribution, with 9 percent supporting students from the highest quintile of income distribution. In secondary education, the share of the public subsidy accruing to students from the two lowest quintiles of household income distribution shrinks to 18 percent. In tertiary education the regressive nature of the public subsidy becomes even starker, with just 3 percent of the public subsidy to tertiary education benefiting students from the poorest two quintiles of income distribution, whereas students from the highest quintile of household income distribution accrue 82 percent of the public subsidy. The unit cost of tertiary education over the unit cost of primary education is alarmingly high, at 225. After the introduction of cost sharing in tertiary education, the Malawian government has supported the provision of loans to tertiary students with a number of loan schemes. However, the recovery of these loans has been generally poor (Hall and Mambo 2015).

Malawi's tertiary gender parity index, at 0.65, is lower than the average for SSA. The University of Malawi applies affirmative action criteria to encourage female enrollment. Recognizing that low female enrollment is in part a consequence of poor facilities to accommodate female students, a number of colleges are in the process of building and renovating accommodations for female students. In Malawi, female students are less likely to enroll in higher education if they are required to leave their home district. As a consequence, Chancellor College will open satellite colleges, in part to facilitate improved female participation. Chancellor College also employs a special needs lecturer, who currently assists 15 enrolled students with disabilities.

Significant disparities are also evident on the basis of location; for example, in 2014 the pupil-teacher ratio for secondary schools in urban areas was 35:1 compared with 50:1 for rural areas (Hall and Mambo 2015).

The Case of Mozambique

In 2013, total education expenditures in Mozambique were equivalent to 6.6 percent of GDP, with the total public allocation for higher education equivalent to 0.9 percent of GDP. In light of the fact that Mozambique is one of the poorest countries in the world, the 13.7 percent of total education spending assigned to higher education is reasonable. In 2013, the GER for secondary education was approximately 26 percent. Poor participation in secondary education underpins low enrollment in tertiary education (Cloete et al. 2011). From a regional perspective, with 496 students enrolled in tertiary education per 100,000 inhabitants in 2013, Mozambique performs poorly compared with Zimbabwe and Botswana, which have 665 and 2,727 students enrolled in tertiary education per 100,000 inhabitants, respectively.

The gender parity index at the tertiary level is about the SSA average. Gender parity is somewhat better in some private institutions than in public universities. Relatively high levels of female enrollment are explained in part by access and affordability, as well as the mix of degrees offered at different institutions.

Medicine, law, and accounting have disproportionately high female enrollment, whereas engineering's share of female enrollment is significantly below average (Brito 2003).

Historically, development has been unevenly concentrated in the southern provinces (Maputo, Gaza, and Inhambane) of the country, compared with the central (Manica, Sofala, Tete, and Zambezia) and northern provinces (Nampula, Niassa, and Cape Delgado). The southern provinces are, moreover, closer to the capital, Maputo, and the regional economic powerhouse South Africa. Enrollment in higher education by residents of the northern and central provinces is much lower than in the southern provinces (Mário et al. 2003).

Mozambique currently has no national financial aid scheme to support students in tertiary education. In 2002, the government introduced the Quality Enhancement and Innovative Facility, a provincial scholarship scheme, which has improved access to higher education for students from poor, rural backgrounds (Bailey, Cloete, and Pillay 2011). Later, scholarship provision expanded to include students enrolled in private higher education.

The Case of Niger

In 2014, 21.7 percent of total government expenditures in Niger were allocated to education, equivalent to 6.8 percent of GDP. Spending in support of education in Niger, as a proportion of GDP, is significantly higher than the average for countries in the region. In 2010, 60 percent of total education spending was assigned to primary education, 25 percent to secondary education, and 12 percent to tertiary education (with the balance of 3 percent allocated to nonformal education).

Access to education in Niger has improved but remains very low and very inequitable. Driven by the imperative to achieve the Millennium Development Goals associated with education, Niger showed significant progress in the period 2001–10, almost doubling the GER for primary education, from 35 to 67 percent (from 29 to 60 percent for female students). Despite these achievements, Niger continues to demonstrate primary and secondary school enrollment rates that are lower than those of every other country in SSA except the Central African Republic. And, although rates of primary enrollment on the part of children from poor households have increased rapidly over the last decade, disparities remain pronounced. In 2011, the GER for secondary education in Niger was 14.4 percent, significantly below the SSA average of 40.4 percent. The GER for upper-secondary education in Niger is even poorer, at 4 percent. The number of students enrolled in higher education per 100,000 inhabitants in Niger was only 123 in 2014, compared with a regional average of 1,212.

As illustrated in table 7.2 below, returns to education in Niger increase with each level of education, with particularly high wage payoffs evident in the transition from secondary to technical and vocational education and training (TVET), and from TVET to higher education (World Bank 2014).

Table 7.2 Income Levels (Hourly FCFA) Dependent on Education and Professional Category

Category	Total	Employed	Self-Employed, Nonagricultural
No schooling	32	72	107
Primary	43	153	161
Secondary	69	277	127
TVET	390	417	264
Higher education	669	669	162

Source: World Bank 2010.
Note: FCFA = West African CFA franc; TVET = technical and vocational education and training.

The Case of Nigeria

On the basis of its commitment to making higher education accessible to all young people, irrespective of socioeconomic status or ethnicity, the government of Nigeria provides free undergraduate education for all students enrolled in federal universities. As a consequence, Nigeria's federal universities rely heavily on government subventions to cover their running costs. However, the magnitude of public transfers is insufficient to cope with increasing demand for higher education, and there is increasing pressure on the government to reform the current policy. Through the National Universities Commission, all federal universities are required to generate 10 percent of their annual funds internally (Jaja 2013).

Admission to higher education in Nigeria is based on a student's performance on the Unified Tertiary Matriculation Examination, administered by the Joint Admission and Matriculation Board. Research suggests that very few prospective students who apply to a university are admitted, with one study reporting that only 5.2–15.3 percent of applicants are admitted every year (Aluede, Idogho, and Imonikhe 2012). Not only are the prospects for admission generally quite narrow but the criteria used for selection are also skewed in favor of certain groups. The federal guidelines for admission into universities prioritize merit (45 percent), catchment area or locality (35 percent), and the promotion of access for students from educationally less-developed states (20 percent). Catchment areas define a geographical area from which a higher educational institution is allowed or obliged to pick candidates (Moti 2010). In practice, the system excludes many worthy candidates and admits many comparatively weak candidates because of their political connectivity or their place of origin (Nwagwu 1997).

Nigeria's gender parity index for enrollment in tertiary education is in line with the SSA average; however, there is a marked underrepresentation of female staff. Female professors constitute only 6.9 percent of total academic staff, and over 70 percent of female professors are concentrated in the humanities (Ogbogu 2009). A number of universities have taken action to address gender imbalance. For example, Obafemi Awolowo University, in partnership with the Carnegie Corporation, has implemented a Gender Equity Project to promote female participation through scholarships for female students, fellowships for female staff, sensitization and advocacy workshops, enlightenment and outreach programs, and networking with universities within and outside Nigeria (Abiose 2008).

The Case of Senegal

In 2011, Senegal allocated 32 percent of its national recurrent budget to the education sector, the highest share of recurrent expenditures dedicated to education for any country in SSA. Higher education receives 24 percent of the education budget, equivalent to 1.2 percent of GDP. As a proportion of GDP, Senegal's spending on higher education is approximately double the SSA average of 0.6 percent, and more than double the South Asian average of 0.5 percent.

Government allocations to higher education institutions (HEIs) are determined on the basis of a negotiated budget. As a consequence, state financing is not linked to institutional performance and can be highly variable, year on year. Government expenditures on public higher education are disproportionately concentrated in support of student subsidies relative to operating expenditures. Between 2005 and 2008, expenditures on student scholarships and other student services accounted for 62 percent of total recurrent expenditures in support of public tertiary education.

In recent years, expenditures on HEIs have consistently exceeded available resources, although deficits are trending downward. Because of the combined pressures of an increasing demand for higher education and an increasingly constrained resource environment, HEIs in Senegal are making increased efforts to raise revenues independent of government allocations. Between 2005 and 2008, university-generated revenue (primarily accounted for by the provision of courses for fees) grew at an annual rate of 12.9 percent, outpacing growth in public financing for the sector (9.8 percent).

A comparison of monthly earnings disaggregated by educational attainment demonstrates that a substantial wage premium accrues to workers who hold a tertiary education. Mean wages increase by approximately 10 percent with each level of educational attainment (primary, secondary, and vocational and technical), with the exception of tertiary education, where the mean wage was double that associated with a general secondary education. Taking into account forgone earnings and private expenditures on education, the private internal rate of return to higher education in Senegal is estimated to be between 12.7 and 17.2 percent, representing, in turn, a strong incentive for individuals to invest in tertiary education.

Inequality in access to public resources leads to significant disparities in education. In 2005, the Gini coefficient for expenditures on higher education in Senegal was 0.59. The number of Senegalese students studying abroad who benefited from public scholarships ballooned from 1,200 in 2000 to 5,600 in 2008. Many of these students were allegedly studying programs available in Senegal and provided by local universities, and only an estimated 5 percent returned to Senegal at the end of their studies.

Internal efficiency in higher education is low. The number of students who enter HEIs and finish their studies within the standard time for the program is very low. Institutional leaders argue that students want to stay in the HEIs as long as possible because they continue to receive a scholarship as long as they are enrolled. Given that many graduates struggle to find employment in the labor market, some students perceive continued enrollment in higher education as a means for earning income. The current government is aware of this problem but has yet to effect any changes, in part because it established the scholarship policy.

The Case of Sierra Leone

Prior to the social upheaval associated with the recent Ebola epidemic, demand for education in Sierra Leone had been consistently high. Increasing demand for education is largely associated with the relative youth of the country's population; approximately 70 percent of inhabitants are under the age of 30, and 40 percent of the overall population falls within the age cohorts associated with early childhood education, basic education, and secondary school, or 3–17 years of age (Guerrero 2014). The improved supply of education over the course of the past decade increased access to education at all levels, especially at postprimary levels. Although Sierra Leone demonstrates low participation in preprimary education, access to primary education is in line with the SSA average. GER for secondary enrollment is higher than for other SSA countries (World Bank 2013).

Enrollment in higher education increased from 8,913 in 2000–01 to 31,103 in 2011–12. Private higher education, in particular, has boomed over the course of the past decade, with the number of private HEIs rising from zero in 2004 to 24 in 2011. Despite improved net enrollment, with an estimated tertiary enrollment of 600 per 100,000 inhabitants in 2011, coverage remains low compared with other countries in the subregion (World Bank 2013).

Between 2004 and 2011, education spending in Sierra Leone was relatively stable; but, at 3.9 percent, spending on education as a share of GDP is low from a regional and SSA perspective. Notwithstanding this observation, the education sector consumes 29 percent of the country's recurrent expenditures, compared with an average of 22 percent in other low-income countries in the region (World Bank 2013).

The government of Sierra Leone has prioritized improved financing of the higher education sector, with a significant increase in funding occurring in 2012 in line with a negotiated salary increase for staff in tertiary institutions. In the period prior to the 2012 increase, public expenditures on tertiary education averaged between 18 and 20 percent of total public expenditures on education. Following the salary increase in 2012, public spending on tertiary education increased to 23 percent of total spending on education (World Bank 2013).

Although female enrollment in higher education is quite low, between 2000 and 2011 the share of female students in public enrollment rose from 29 to 36 percent (Guerrero 2014). The gender parity index is 0.79, relatively high within the subregional group. Although the Ebola outbreak negatively affected all education in Sierra Leone, it had a pronounced impact on female education. Families that lost a breadwinner are unable to afford food, let alone fees to support education. As a consequence, many children have been withdrawn from school to make money for the family, and this has resulted in a higher incidence of teenage pregnancy (Bordner 2016).

From an equity perspective, disparities in tertiary education in Sierra Leone are largely accounted for by relative household wealth and location. The 2011 Sierra Leone Integrated Household Survey demonstrated that only 0.4 percent of the poorest segment of the population and 1 percent of the rural population are enrolled in higher education. However, the survey showed that 13.4 percent of the richest segment of the population, and 9.9 percent of urban residents, were enrolled in higher education (Guerrero 2014). All four regions of the country host at least one public HEI, but these are primarily located in larger towns. Private HEIs are primarily located in urban centers, in particular in Freetown, the capital city (World Bank 2013). Half of the country's 14 districts, including most of the rural districts, do not have a tertiary education institution (Guerrero 2014).

Sierra Leonean students must graduate from secondary school with a credit pass in at least five subjects for admission to a university, or four subjects for admission to other tertiary institutions. In many instances, institutions require that credit passes include English language and mathematics. The number of Sierra Leonean candidates sitting for the West African Senior School Certificate Examination (WASSCE) quadrupled between 2003 and 2011, rising from 11,135 students to 44,790. However, pass rates (defined as a credit pass in at least four subjects) remain very low; in 2011 only 10 percent of students who sat for the WASSCE passed the exam, and only 5 percent of students passed mathematics, which is a requirement for entry to a university (World Bank 2013). Students from rural areas and poor districts, where the quality of teaching and teaching materials are generally poor, perform particularly poorly on the WASSCE.

All students enrolled in higher education in Sierra Leone are expected to pay fees. The government administers a system of grants to support students in tertiary education, but the process of allocating these grants lacks transparency. The grants are meant to be allocated in line with district quotas and other quotas that apply to each institution, but it is unclear how these are determined (World Bank 2013). Decisions on the awarding of the grants are made in Freetown, with the minister of education giving the final approval (Guerrero 2014).

Higher education graduates in Sierra Leone are primarily employed in professional, technical, and managerial jobs (61 percent of male and 67 percent of female graduates), and are less likely to be employed in the agricultural sector than other workers with lower educational attainment. This is especially true for female higher education graduates; although 57 percent of the female labor force with less than tertiary educational attainment works in the agricultural sector, just 0.9 percent of female workers with a tertiary qualification are employed in agriculture. Moreover, only 6 percent of women without higher education work in a professional, technical, or managerial position, compared with 36.5 and 67 percent of male and female workers, respectively, who hold a tertiary qualification (World Bank 2013).

The Case of Uganda

In 2013, total expenditures in support of education in Uganda were equivalent to 2.2 percent of GDP, with the share allocated to higher education equivalent to approximately 0.3 percent of GDP. These figures are low both from a regional perspective and in comparison to other developing countries. In the Ugandan education system as a whole, lower educational levels account for the majority of education spending. With population growth equivalent to approximately 3.6 percent per year and the national fertility rate at 6.7 children per woman, despite the achievement of universal primary education, the costs of delivering lower levels of education will continue to rise in alignment with an expanding youth population (Nannyonjo, Mulindwa, and Usher 2009).

Access to public higher education is based on a dual-track admissions policy, in which the government supports the costs of 4,000 students, approximately one-quarter of total university enrollment. Students supported by the government exclusively attend public universities, and the government finances all of their costs (tuition fees and room and board). This practice is justified on the basis that it meets the needs of the national economy and addresses the issue of equity in higher education. Students who do not receive government sponsorship finance their own education. Eighty percent of students at Makerere University pay for their tuition, and this source of revenue accounts for more than half of the university's total revenue (Musisi and Muwanga 2003). Each faculty sets the tuition fees for students admitted through the private entry scheme, which is subject to the approval of the Academic Senate and the University Council. Fees vary by faculty, with sciences tending to charge more than humanities faculties. The council is generally reluctant to approve tuition increases because of fears of student unrest.

The government of Uganda has stated its intention to reduce income inequality. In higher education, the government has highlighted the need to expand access for students from poorer backgrounds (Nannyonjo, Mulindwa, and Usher 2009). Despite this intention, the 4,000 students admitted on government scholarships are disproportionately representative of wealthy households, with parents who are more likely to have paid for expensive secondary schools where tuition can be more expensive than that charged by a university. From an equity perspective, the wrong students are being supported with public money to attend higher education. The challenge of identifying bright but needy students for admission to higher education remains unsolved (Nannyonjo, Mulindwa, and Usher 2009).

References

Abiose, S. 2008. "Gender Policy for Obafemi Awolowo University." *OAU-Carnegie Gender Equity Initiative Bulletin* 6 (1): 2–3.

Aluede, O., P. O. Idogho, and J. S. Imonikhe. 2012. "Increasing Access to University Education in Nigeria: Present Challenges and Suggestions for the Future." *The African Symposium* 12 (2).

Amburo, A. P. 2011. *Teaching in a Changing Africa: Differential Academic Performance of Students from Academies and Public Primary Schools at KCSE Examination in Kenya*. Narok, Kenya: Narok University College.

Anyan, J. 2011. *Dealing with Higher Education Exclusion in Ghana: Why the Secondary School Factor Matters*. Helsinki: University of Helsinki.

Bailey, Tracy, Nico Cloete, and Pundy Pillay. 2011. "Case Study: Mozambique and Eduardo Mondlane University." Centre for Higher Education Trust, Wynberg, Cape Town.

Bordner, A. T. 2016. "Post-Ebola Challenges for Education in West Africa." World Education News & Reviews, September 8. http://wenr.wes.org/2015/09/post-ebola-challenges-education-west-africa.

Brito, L. 2003. *The Mozambican Experience: Initiating and Sustaining Tertiary Education Reform*. Maputo: Ministry for Higher Education, Science and Technology, Mozambique.

Cloete, N., T. Bailey, P. Pillay, I. Bunting, and P. Maassen. 2011. *Universities and Economic Development in Africa*. Wynberg, South Africa: Centre for Higher Education Transformation (CHET).

DPMF (Development Policy Management Forum). 2012. *Brief Profile of Inequality in Kenya*. from DPMF (accessed December 22, 2014), http://www.dpmf.org/dpmf/index.php?option=com_content&view=article&id=97: a-brief-general-profile-on-inequality-inkenya&catid=43: social-policy-development-and-governance-in-kenya&Itemid=94.

Guerrero, C. 2014. "Higher Education Case Studies: Sierra Leone." The Economist Intelligence Unit, London.

Hall, N., and M. Mambo. 2015. "Financing Education in Malawi: Opportunities for Action: Country Case Study for the Oslo Summit on Education for Development." Education for Development Summit, Oslo, July 6–7.

Jaja, J. M. 2013. "Higher Education in Nigeria: Its Gain, Its Burden." *Global Journal of Human Social Science: Linguistics & Education* 13 (14).

Marcucci, P. N. 2007. "Tuition Policies in a Comparative Perspective: Theoretical and Political Rationales." *Journal of Higher Education Policy and Management* 29 (1): 25–40.

Mário, M., P. Fry, L. Levey, and A. Chilundo. 2003. *Higher Education in Mozambique: A Case Study*. New York: Partnership for Higher Education in Africa.

Morley, L., F. Leach, R. Lugg, E. Bhalalusesa, R. Mwaipopo, L. Dzama Forde, and G. Egbanya. 2007. *Widening Participation in Higher Education in Ghana and Tanzania: Developing an Equity Scorecard*. Brighton: University of Sussex (U.K.) Centre for Higher Education & Equity.

Moti, U. G. 2010. "The Challenges of Access to University Education in Nigeria." *DSM Business Review* 2 (2): 27–56.

Mulongo, G. 2013. "Inequality in Accessing Higher Education in Kenya; Implications for Economic Development and Well-Being." *International Journal of Humanities and Social Science* 3 (16).

Musisi, N., and N. K. Muwanga. 2003. *Makerere University in Transition 1993–2000: Opportunities and Challenges*. New York: Partnership for Higher Education in Africa.

Mwiria, K., and N. Ng'ethe. 2002. "Public University Reform in Kenya: Mapping the Key Changes of the Last Decade." Unpublished research report, Nairobi.

Nannyonjo, Harriet, Innocent Najjumba Mulindwa, and Alex Usher. 2009. *Funding Higher Education in Uganda in an Era of Growth*. Washington, DC: World Bank.

Ngome, C. 2003. "Kenya." In *African Higher Education: An International*, edited by D. Teferra, and P. G. Altbach, 359–71. Bloomington: Indiana University Press.

Nwagwu, C. C. 1997. "The Environment of Crises in the Nigerian Education System." *Comparative Education* 33 (1): 87–95.

Ogbogu, C. 2009. "An Analysis of Female Research Productivity in Nigerian Universities." *Journal of Higher Education Policy and Management* 31 (1): 17–22.

Otieno, W. 2004. "Student Loans in Kenya: Past Experiences, Current Hurdles, and Opportunities for the Future." *JHEA/RESA* 2 (2): 75–99.

World Bank. 2010. *Improving Education and Developing Skills for Economic Growth in Niger*. Washington, DC: World Bank.

———. 2013. *Republic of Burundi Public Expenditure Review: Strengthening Fiscal Resilience to Promote Government Effectiveness*. Washington, DC: World Bank.

———. 2014. *Project Appraisal Document*. Washington, DC: World Bank. http://documents.worldbank.org/curated/en/671631468292230996/pdf/PAD4440PAD0P1324050Box382141B00PUBLIC0.pdf.

———. 2015. *Africa's Pulse*. Washington, DC: World Bank.

Environmental Benefits Statement

The World Bank Group is committed to reducing its environmental footprint. In support of this commitment, we leverage electronic publishing options and print-on-demand technology, which is located in regional hubs worldwide. Together, these initiatives enable print runs to be lowered and shipping distances decreased, resulting in reduced paper consumption, chemical use, greenhouse gas emissions, and waste.

We follow the recommended standards for paper use set by the Green Press Initiative. The majority of our books are printed on Forest Stewardship Council (FSC)–certified paper, with nearly all containing 50–100 percent recycled content. The recycled fiber in our book paper is either unbleached or bleached using totally chlorine-free (TCF), processed chlorine-free (PCF), or enhanced elemental chlorine-free (EECF) processes.

More information about the Bank's environmental philosophy can be found at http://www.worldbank.org/corporateresponsibility.

 www.ingramcontent.com/pod-product-compliance
Lightning Source LLC
Chambersburg PA
CBHW060316240426
43661CB00059B/2780